GRIT UNDER MY NAILS

*One woman's extraordinary journey to discover that it's all possible.
Including survival.*

A MEMOIR IN THREE ACTS
HENDA SALMERON

Grit Under My Nails
Henda Salmeron

Copyright © 2018 Jabulani House
www.HendaSalmeron.com

JABULANI
HOUSE

All rights reserved. No part of this book may be used or reproduced without written permission from the author, except in the case of brief quotations.

FLUENCY
TELLING STORIES THAT MATTER

Produced with the assistance of Fluency Organization, Inc.
Graphic design: Inkwell Creative
Cover: André Provedel
Photographer: Greg Blomberg

Excerpt from A NEW PATH TO THE WATERFALL, copyright © 1989 by the Estate of Raymond Carver. Used by permission of Grove/Atlantic, Inc. Any third party use of this material, outside of this publication, is prohibited.

"The Horse" by Ronald Duncan © (copyright of) the Ronald Duncan Estate. Used with permission.

Printed in the United States of America

To Mateo and Dominique. I love you.

To Mary Ann and Bruce. Simply with sincere gratitude.

Dear Stranger and Friend,
It took more than two years to tell you my story. I spent countless solitary nights at my kitchen counter reliving years of heartbreak. But in the telling and the sharing, my healing began. I desired from the start to gain clarity, reach acceptance, and be free from the weight. Thank you for coming along and listening.

A portion of the net proceeds from the sale of this book will be donated to charity.

ACT 1: BEFORE CANCER

Scene 1	America the Beautiful!	9
Scene 2	Down Memory Lane We Waltz	14
Scene 3	Launching My Fourth-Grade 1976 Escape Pod	18
Scene 4	Happy Fifteenth Birthday to Me!	20
Scene 5	The People I Love—Then, Now, and Always	25
Scene 6	Comfort Food	30
Scene 7	In the Presence of Greatness	34
Scene 8	Emerging from My Chrysalis	40
Scene 9	Butterfly Days	45
Scene 10	Exit Stage Left, 1990	49
Scene 11	Oh Africa, My Africa!	51
Scene 12	Wedding Bells Are Ringing!	55
Scene 13	Friday the 13th, June 1995	59
Scene 14	Building with Blocks	61
Scene 15	South African Homecoming	64
Scene 16	Augury in Pink, Late Summer 2008	66
Scene 17	The Messenger	68

ACT 2: CANCER

Scene 1	East Texas in Springtime	73
Scene 2	One Traveling Bandaged Dense Breast, Late July 2009	85
Scene 3	My Not-So-Finest Hour Eating Darn Fine BBQ!	91
Scene 4	When Lightning Strikes	95
Scene 5	The Stink of Fear	99
Scene 6	The Accidental Making of a Lobbyist	101

ACT 3: AFTER CANCER

Scene 1	Arising from the Ashes	109
Scene 2	Patience, Grasshopper! (Master Po, Kung Fu)	113

Scene 3	Wilderness Musings	117
Scene 4	Curbside Bulk Trash Pick-Up	122
Scene 5	Wondrous Love	129
Scene 6	Indian Rhapsody	135
Scene 7	Abode of Snow	138
Scene 8	One Hundred and Thirty-Two Hours Later	143
Scene 9	Titans Awake!	147
Scene 10	Spilling Secrets	149
Scene 11	Per Angusta Ad Augusta	152
Scene 12	Aftershock	155
Scene 13	Silk and Spice and Everything Nice	157
Scene 14	Charging Hell with a Bucket of Ice Water	161
Scene 15	Searching for a Whisper in a Whirlwind	164
Scene 16	One-Legged at a Butt-Kicking Convention	167
Scene 17	Possum Pie for Dinner	171
Scene 18	Hauling Ass	173
Scene 19	One Wheel Down and the Axle Dragging	177
Scene 20	The Morning After	183
Scene 21	Solo and Filled with Sorrow	187
Scene 22	Without a Fight	193
Scene 23	The Crash of 2012	195
Scene 24	Under a Desert Sky	200
Scene 25	Love Unleashed	205
Scene 26	Dining at Nature's Enchanted Buffet	210
Scene 27	Costa Rica Heartbreak Hotel	213
Scene 28	The Sucking Dating Games	217
Scene 29	Namaste—The Spirit within Me Sees the Spirit in You	223
Scene 30	Pegasus	229
Scene 31	The Great Deportation Recap	233
Scene 32	The Power of Purple	237
Scene 33	Free Dog	241

EPILOGUE

My Name Is Grace 245

ACT 1

BEFORE CANCER

The key to immortality is first living a life worth remembering.

—ST. AUGUSTINE, ABOUT 1,600 YEARS AGO

America the Beautiful!

I KNOW IT'S NONE of my business how you hang your toilet paper. It's your bathroom. Clearly, as your visitor, you would be quite horrified knowing that I'm changing your toilet paper around. I'm sorry. This is way too much information. But it drives me nuts when the paper is under and not over. If I go back to the dinner table without switching it around, I would be unable to focus on the conversation. All I would see is your upside-down roll. For the sake of successive disclosure, I also change the toilet rolls on airplanes, in restaurants, hotels, and public bathrooms. Apparently research shows 70% of people like their paper to be over, although the other 30% does it under. It seems as "under," it has less chance of unrolling during an earthquake or in an RV going down the road!

When you walk next to me, I will keep switching you if you wander to my left side. That's my spot. My energy just doesn't feel right when I'm on your inside. Even though it's a gentleman thing to protect a woman from oncoming cars. It's okay. I won't think less of you. And if we don't switch, I again will be too distracted to focus on your company.

As a South African with plenty of bush smarts, I consider myself an authority on the fine art of squatting while watching out for a lion and keeping my shoes dry. I also have special skills slurping marrow from shanks and other bones. In restaurants I will restrain my undomesticated side and use utensils to get every buttery morsel. Otherwise I have no problem digging in with both hands and scraping the bones clean. I have lived in Dallas, Texas, since 1994 and am happy that there are a couple of local restaurants serving simply roasted marrowbones.

Despite a quarter-century of calling the great United States home, my Texas lingo is limited to "y'all" and "git 'er done." I could never pass for a local in the Lone Star State. On any trip to West Texas I leave the talking up to other people. My teenage kids often question the credentials of my computer science degree, partly due to my complete lack of understanding their math or science homework. It does make one speculate whether I bought the certificate on eBay. Undeniably I would fail miserably if I had to try to pass ninth grade today. But cut me some slack, as I didn't speak English until I was about nineteen years old! Our English as a Second Language reads in high school were limited to Shakespeare. Therefore my American illiteracy extends to the great and legendary American authors. One day I will read them all—I promise. Until then at least my accent leads people to think I'm well educated and that I speak proper English. Ha! If only they knew Google and I are practically family, and Wikipedia is named in my will. Thank God for Al Gore inventing the Information Super Highway!

My red, white, and blue voyage launched on a very cold winter's eve in December 1990 when I checked into the Holiday Inn across from the Winston-Salem Coliseum in North Carolina. I arrived on American soil with two suitcases, each weighing about forty-four pounds, $1,500 in my pocket, and a work visa. I also had a bottle of fine 1966 Portuguese port—my birth year and a farewell present from a longtime friend. And I was very alone. I might as well have been dropped off on a deserted beach in the South Pacific. Without family and no friends in the Western Hemisphere, I was my own island. Please remember this was in prehistoric times—pre-cell phone invasion, before texting, no Facebook affection, and Twitter was still merely a bird sound!

Another South African (and soon-to-be colleague) picked me up from the airport. Indian outsourcing didn't exist then, and South Africa had plenty of English-proficient computer programmers. Of course some of us pretended to be more versed in English than we really were, if you get my drift. We were willing to work for less than our American counterparts in exchange for a work visa. My colleague and I were both headhunted by a New York firm and placed with RJ Reynolds Tobacco in North Carolina. With no family to tie me down, closing shop in South Africa was a speedy affair. When I accepted the job offer, I had no foggy clue where North Carolina was. A borrowed, out-of-date *Britannica Encyclopedia* confirmed it was part of the southern States. Okay, sounded peachy. Honestly, I didn't really care where it was because I was coming to America!

My relocation package included a seven-day hotel stay during which time I had to find a place to live. I still reminisce over my initial trip to K-Mart to buy all the household basics of starting over. Wow!

What an amazing place—and so cheap! I had never seen so many choices. Carless growing up, I was also utterly speechless when I could buy a real car, a golden 1970 Chevette, for $350. Okay, fine… in hindsight it was a piece of total junk. It was without a working speedometer and emergency brake. The radio worked, the AC worked sometimes, and the engine had the rasping coughs of a chain-smoking sailor. Six months later when I donated it for scrap metal, I unlovingly referred to it as my Shi*vette.

On a tight budget, finding affordable housing was paramount. I was overjoyed when I located an apartment with a fitness center, pool, tennis court, and party room. Two days after moving in all the pipes burst from a winter ice storm. I had to crash on the couch of my South African coworker and newfound best friend. What a pity I missed the part that it was on the wrong side of town. Hence the cheap price! In complete disbelief, I discovered the next day that my apartment building had been raided overnight by a bunch of delinquents. They stole everything I owned. Everything. All my groceries and all my clothes, including my underwear and shoes. I mean seriously, who steals other people's cotton underwear and used shoes? They took my brand-new bed sheets, towels, pillows, blankets, my two suitcases, and my 1966 bottle of port! Okay, I get the port part, but I'm still dumbstruck to this day about my underwear.

I grew up in one of the most dangerous countries on the planet. Like an American seven-layer dip for a Super Bowl party, our houses had eight-foot walls, barbwire, electric fencing, burglar bars, panic buttons, guard dogs, and private security patrols. Seven days after arriving in the safety of the USA, without renter insurance, my American dream was in shambles. I just had the clothes I was wearing and $200 cash. My employer offered to advance me $1,000 and although grateful, I knew it would not stretch very far. Even with shopping at K-Mart!

The generosity of strangers rescued me. Learning about my loss, my boss, a short Italian originally from New York City, took me to his house during lunchtime. There I met his wife. Bedridden, she had advanced multiple sclerosis and could no longer walk. She opened her closets and invited me to help myself. In lieu of my early 1990s neon and shoulder pads, for the first few months I could easily have been mistaken for a character from the 1970s *Mary Tyler Moore Show*. My period clothing fit perfectly with my car's bygone era. I sported A-line skirts with turtlenecks and double-breasted wool coats. My brightly colored Crimplene tailored suits (a.k.a. polyester!) matched my floral-patterned pussy bow blouses. I completed my Seventies impersonation by adding some matching eyeshadow in shimmering shades of lilac, green, and baby blue. I am eternally grateful for the hand-me-downs and will never forget this woman's kindness.

In my borrowed clothes I was ready to blend stars and stripes into my mix. Upon learning that I was from the southern tip of Africa, most greeted me with, "How come you're not black?!" My American vision demanded the conversion of Henda, the Afrikaans Boer girl, to some local flavor. I learned to embrace pepperoni pizza, Dr Pepper, American football, corn dogs, and fried fruit pies. Furthermore, my concocted story about my origins was also shaping up nicely. My rehearsed lines about my past rang true, even to myself. I was an orphan, wasn't I?

Down Memory Lane We Waltz

THE FIRST TENDER GREENS of spring shyly revealed themselves after their winter pause. It was as if they threw off their cold clothes overnight for the spunky yellow-green jackets of the season. The white blossoms of the Bradford pear trees lined the streets like young blushing brides dressed in their snowy wedding gowns, filled with promise and the hope of new beginnings. I respected their daring as the threat of a late frost, ready to extinguish their exuberant color, was still possible. Each spring I'm reminded that I too can shed my burden for a fresh start. The promise of rebirth. How sweet is the power that we, like nature each year, can start anew?

Although I value all the seasons, springtime commands my full attention. Pretoria, my hometown growing up and the jacaranda capital, was draped every spring in waves of lavender. The jacaranda trees all over the city exploded with a joyous burst, spilling their delicate bell-shaped flowers abundantly. It was a celebration, a colorful display of nature's most extravagant spring show. Lore had it that when strolling with your much-loved down the amethyst-swathed streets, true devotion was promised if a single petal landed, unassisted, on your head.

I hate the color purple. I tell my kids frequently that "hate" is a strong word and we must be very careful when we use it. But I can say with certainty that I hate purple. Not the shades of lavender, lilac, amethyst, or mauve. To be exact, I despise the deep purple associated with royalty, Mardi Gras, and Lent. It is the earliest memory I have.

She wore a purple dress with a matching hat, and we stood next to an open grave. I was three years old, and I recall watching people toss rose petals on the casket down below. A gust of wind blew her hat into the grave. It softly landed on the flowers inside the coffin. The hat was buried with the dead that day. I often wonder how long it took for the purple fibers to crumble and mix with the earth. I ponder if the wire that kept the hat's shape is still there, or if it also became dust. For many years I thought my father was laid to rest that day. My life was interrupted for the first time and my destiny's course altered, one of many times to come.

A homeless man lives on a bus bench near my current home in Dallas. He closely guards a shopping cart holding his meager belongings. I saw him repeatedly during the past winter, and for his sake I was glad the threat of cold and freezing nights had passed. I felt guilty every time I saw his downward gaze that I made neither the time nor the priority to learn his name and story. He reminded me of a spring that would not return as he had surrendered to a stark grey and hopeless existence.

I could so easily have chosen to call a bus bench home. It was a small marvel that I made it through childhood and my teenage years with no needle marks on my arms. I had no outward scars to tell the grim story of how I felt the necessity to put the Atlantic Ocean between myself and this woman. I hesitate to call her "Mother," as the word implies protector and nurturer. After the funeral she gave her older three kids to the dead man's family and the youngest two, including me, to the neighbors. Then she just vanished. Don't you give puppies away? Or old clothes? Certainly not your kids. I have no recollection of my earliest years in this family's loving care, although in due course they became an integral part of my existence. The distress I still feel today when I see that exact shade of purple underscores how bottomless my wounds were.

I only remember when she came to get me two years later—she came back and didn't forget me! I was five years old when she took me with her. My younger half-brother stayed behind with the neighbors for the time being. We lived together in a tiny single-room boarding house in a small town near Johannesburg where she was a receptionist. We shared a narrow bed and made tea and coffee using hot water from the tap in the communal bathroom down the hall. Cockroaches were our unwelcomed roommates. She hardly had enough money to feed us, but it didn't matter because we were together.

Within a few months we moved to Pretoria. I was in kindergarten, and my mother still worked as a receptionist by day and pursued the nonstop struggle to land a man by night. Our small one-room flat severely limited privacy of any kind. Her boyfriends stayed over repeatedly. I learned early to pretend being fast asleep in my single bed adjacent to hers. The grown-up expression of passion was foreign to my ears. I didn't quite grasp why it sounded like she was being hurt over and over. But I kept quiet, as it was the smart thing to do.

She sought my advice frequently. When asking a six-year-old her opinion about the company of the men you keep, you must be prepared for simple assessments. One of them was unforgettable. He had a red face, was not nice, and smelled sour all the time, and I intuitively distrusted him. I even suggested that she kick him out. She was completely adrift in the struggle to make a living in the big city and leaned on me as her guidance counselor and confidant. I knew no better and gladly stepped into the role of "mother."

In first grade I swiftly discovered my flair to blend in. I attended an affluent public elementary school near our flat and quickly learned that no one really cared beyond what you chose to share. There is a difference between lying and just not telling. I could assess any situation swiftly and was able to think on my feet. My status of star student and teacher's pet was the perfect cover for a kid caught in the crosshairs of being mature beyond my years in a home that left a lot to be desired.

I was also introduced to the first chapter of shame. I was ashamed of my mother. I was ashamed of the terrible place where we lived. I was ashamed that I didn't have a father. I compared myself to the other kids and I didn't feel I was good enough. Welcome to my lifelong chapter about my unworthiness. But I was proud to be one of the top students and discovered academics as the great equalizer between the haves and have-nots. It saved me from the bus bench.

My mother was a petite and slim woman. When her tummy grew, it was very hard to hide it from people, especially me. A baby was developing inside her. It didn't take long to realize that another person would soon be sharing our small space. There was much commotion when she almost died from an infection after her backstreet abortion failed. She gave birth to my baby half-sister a few months later during a spectacular lavender spring in Pretoria. What a dilemma, like all unwanted pregnancies always are. She didn't have the luxury of a long maternity break; she had to work to keep a roof over our heads.

When my second-grade classes ended at 2:00 P.M., I would hurry home to relieve the babysitter. I lived in the 1970s South Africa, reminiscent of the American Wild West. Back then nobody queried the sanity of someone allowing an eight-year-old to care for a newborn several hours a day. For me it was a dream come true—my very own live doll to feed, bathe, dress, play with, and adore completely. Her name was Tanja, and she lived with us for more than a year. I still hear her soft baby giggles when a light breeze tickles the blossoms until they cannot help falling to the ground.

Launching My Fourth-Grade 1976 Escape Pod

LIFE CHANGED SUDDENLY. I was not the inner circle confidant I thought I was when dear Mama agreed to marry the man who got her pregnant. What a snake he was! I called him the Creep. But like all creeps, he proved to be a supreme coward. His house was about forty-five minutes from Pretoria and instinct cautioned me not to live there after their speedy courthouse wedding. The Creep made the marriage conditional on giving up our baby girl for adoption. Jerk. She was given to some nice family, and I was left stuck in our not so happily ever after. I can only trust that she lived a charmed existence with little shadows and negligible heartache surrounded by much love, joy, and happiness. After Mother's marriage, my half-brother joined our blissful little brigade. Two years younger than me, he required much more care than she was willing to invest.

My great distraction was my books, whose stories transported me to faraway locations. Their promise of adventure fueled the craving for discovering these places in person one day. I enjoyed reading the *Maasdorp* Afrikaans series by Stella Blakemore written around 1932. The twelve books followed the lives of a group of young girls in boarding school. The main character, Kobie Malan, had golden curls, sapphire blue eyes, cute dimples, and was popular among her teachers and friends. In my imaginary world I quickly became one of the sisterhood. That was it—Plan B! Going away to boarding school was my ticket out of the Creep's house. It took little effort to convince dearest Mother to send me away so she could enjoy her newfound bliss with her charming knight in rotten armor. The extra bonus? The school accepted my half-brother too! Unlike their American and European counterparts, boarding schools in South Africa were not reserved for the elite and wealthy. With distances great and schools limited, boarding schools were common, particularly in the more rural areas. As it was the apartheid years, these schools were reserved for white kids only.

I thrived at boarding school, as I felt safe and secure. My once-chaotic days became a regimen arranged by ringing bells. I slept in dormitories with other girls, many whom were also unwanted. My teachers became my mentors and role models, and with their guidance and nurturing, a rookie leader emerged.

My grades put me on the honor roll, and the last four years of primary school passed quickly with little incident. During this time I discovered my talent for sport. With good hand-eye coordination, balance, and agility, netball became my game. It is a sport like basketball and I represented my province two years in a row. Together with my grades, my sport performance allowed me to be accepted as a full-scholarship boarding student at the best and most prestigious Afrikaans girls high school in South Africa.

Located in Pretoria, this high school for the well-to-do attracted many very privileged kids from wealthy and prominent families. Several of my friends' dads were ambassadors and other high-profile individuals in South Africa. I never mentioned my scholarship status. I was also mute about me not being part of a loving family. After years of practicing hiding my shame, I was an authority in the art of pretending. My shape-shifting aptitude shined brightly, as I was friends with the smart girls, the sport girls, the naughty girls, and some of the bad girls. Me? I comfortably identified with the "cool nerd" role. In the safety of this all-girls' environment, my confidence to lead flourished. During my last two years in high school I was elected to the position of prefect and boarding school Head Girl (à la Harry Potter).

Happy Fifteenth Birthday to Me!

I'M GRIPPING THE SCISSORS *tightly in my right hand. The cold blades resting against my cheek give me reassurance that I'm not defenseless. I can hear him outside my window in the bushes. Although my light is off and I'm lying dead still in the dark, I still feel as if his eyes can see through my curtains. I have the urge to run into the shower and cleanse myself from his filthy stares.*

With absolute certainty, I will not hesitate to use these scissors if he dares to come near me. Although slight, my body is fit from years of athletic participation. I will fight him with every ounce of strength I possess. He picked the wrong kid to mess with. Lying in bed I can feel adrenaline surge through me. I wonder if this was what a soldier feels like before battle or an animal defending itself to the end. Mother is sound asleep. As usual she is oblivious to the absolute terror I encounter every time I set foot in this house.

I have become more at risk. Tonight he walked naked from their bedroom to his study through the room where I was watching TV. He made sure he was in full view behind his desk while he played with himself. I would not show any sign that I noticed he was not wearing pants. He can screw himself. This weekend is the last time I will ever sleep here. I'd rather live under a bridge.

Over the course of the past two years, as my body matured, his lustful stare followed my every movement. Recently his disturbing behavior escalated. I caught him trying to look through the bathroom window while I was taking a bath. Then his nightly visits outside my bedroom window followed. Taking scissors to bed has become part of my nighttime ritual. As has moving my nightstand against the closed door so I will wake if he tries to enter my bedroom.

It's laughable if not so very tragic how more than three decades later this incident is still freshly painted in the present tense. Although not generally superstitious, I do like the imagery that my birth year enjoys in the Chinese Zodiac. I was born in 1966—the year of the Fire Horse. The ancient Chinese fretted about girls born under this sign because of the strength of their power. Many were killed, as it was considered bad luck to have a Fire Horse girl under your roof. Referenced in Japan as *Hinoe-Uma,* the birthrate for girls sharply dropped and the abortion rate increased in 1966. Who knows whether I would have been better off growing up in Asia. I do think I was switched in the hospital and was supposed to go home with the nice normal family—the one with a house, a car, two dogs, and a cat.

With each passing year the relationship with the woman who birthed me deteriorated more. The Creep outdid himself in his slithering skills. Not only did he try to swallow me with his stares, but he also treated her like garbage. My own coat of arms was comprised of "cold, resolute, fearless and total bitch." Neither one of them ever realized the superhuman effort it took as a young teenager to raise it in their presence.

Funny story. She forgot my birthday a few years in a row while growing up. It prompted me to add "having a kid's birthday party" to my bucket list. On August 9, 1990, my work colleagues and friends threw a 24th surprise party for me in Johannesburg. I had a Teenage Mutant Ninja Turtle cake with all the party favors, snacks, and games that any ten-year-old could imagine. It remains my best birthday party ever!

"I don't care and it doesn't matter" was my nightly lullaby. She never saw me cry. I hid the depth of the well of my tears from everybody, including me. She read her Bible all day and carried it around like an amulet to guard her from all wrongdoing. She confessed her "devotion for Jesus" to anybody within earshot and prayed several times a day. Based on her eloquent quotes from the Bible, God would punish me for not showing her the respect the Bible demanded of a child to her parent. Per Mother, I was going straight to hell. Between you and me, I look forward to the conversation with God in person about the double standard. No kid should be expected to honor a parent who put her in such harm's way. In my book, respect and trust are earned. Period.

The unintended consequences of an all-girls' school and growing up without a male role model? My complete naïveté about all things "men." Initially I felt so ashamed of the Creep's unwanted attention. I felt as if I was at fault. Did I trigger his sick behavior? I was confused about what to do. When I had the courage to bring it up to Mother,

I was greeted by outrage. Apparently I was "making it all up" out of jealousy over her happiness. According to her my overactive imagination had fabricated lies to break up their marriage. Evidently I was an unstable and disturbed fifteen-year-old kid. I think all my teachers would have strongly disagreed with her. They commended me for the leadership qualities and academic excellence I exhibited. But then they were unaware their star student had considered stabbing someone with a pair of scissors repeatedly. Maybe she had a point.

Ayn Rand largely influenced me during this time. I completely embraced her philosophy of Objectivism and the notion that we, as flawed humans, were heroic. As a fan, I subscribed to the Ayn Rand Institute and owned all her books. *Atlas Shrugged* and *The Fountainhead* became my moral compasses. Looking back, I should be grateful I didn't follow through to tattoo John Galt's pledge on my thighs: *I swear, by my life and my love of it, that I will never live for the sake of another man, nor ask another man to live for mine.* Yup. I was content to be fully in charge of my own happiness.

I have very few items left from my childhood, but my collection of Ayn Rand's books has followed me across the globe and holds a prime spot on my bookcase. Forty years later, their pages are frail and yellowed with broken spines, and I struggle to read the fine print without reading glasses. Walking by them daily reminds me how much I want to be brave enough to lead with my heart. I want to be unapologetic about any tear-streaked mascara cheeks I entertain.

How could she not believe me? What about me was not worth loving more than some man who was scum? I will never understand the choice she made. Like standing again at an open grave, I felt once more left behind—unwanted and discarded. The anguish has softened over time but its cruel scar will never completely fade. What a phenomenal role model Mother became! All I had to do was put the word "not" in front of her name. My own trademarks became fighter, chameleon, and survivor. Little could I foresee that these early lessons I acquired would later serve as supreme guideposts when I needed them most.

I stand in a land of roses,
But I dream of a land of snow,
Where you and I were happy,
In the years of long ago.
Nightingales in the branches,
Stars in the magic skies,
But I only hear you singing,
I only see your eyes.

Come! come! come to me Thora,
Come once again and be
Child of my dream, light of my life,
Angel of love to me!

I stand again in the North land,
But in silence and in shame;
Your grave is my only landmark,
And men have forgotten my name.
'Tis a tale that is truer and older
Than any the sagas tell,
I lov'd you in life too little,
I love you in death too well.

Speak! speak! speak to me Thora,
Speak from your Heav'n to me;
Child of my dream, love of my life,
Hope of my world to be!

—"THORA," FREDERIC EDWARD WEATHERLY

The People I Love—Then, Now, and Always

My name is Henda... like Honda but with an "e." No, no—not "Honde," as that means "dogs" in Afrikaans! When I order Starbucks, or put my name on a restaurant's waiting list, I often become "Linda," "Glenda," or just plain "huh?" Translated "grace" in Yiddish and the verb "to happen" in Icelandic, my name does not allow me much anonymity in cyberspace. A few keystrokes on Google will lay out a roadmap for any stranger wanting information about me. However, our online personas are just one facet of the sum of our parts. To really know me you must peel back my layers—spend time with me, talk to me, and listen to the story that is uniquely mine.

December always arrived with a sharper edge. It was the high noon of summer south of the equator, and my boarding school closed for several weeks, signaling the end of the school year. The long summer break brought a dilemma, as I had nowhere to go. Staying with Mother and the Creep was as appetizing as leftover cat food. Luckily I had a standing invitation from the people who lovingly took me in when I was a little girl. Gert and Lenie had lived in the coal-mining town of Orkney and were close friends with Mother and her first husband. The two couples had been neighbors and fishing buddies, and typical of small towns, the families spent a lot of time together. My young tongue struggled with "Lenie," and she forever became "Nienie" to me. I shudder to think what could have happened if Gert and Nienie hadn't agreed to take me in after Mother's husband died when I was a toddler.

Later, while I was at boarding school, they retired and moved to a small farming town called Makwassie. It was about three hours northwest of Johannesburg and as flat as West Texas. Mother gladly shipped my younger half-brother and me off to them for every summer vacation. Due to the racial unrest during the late 1970s, it was always an angst-filled eight-hour journey unaccompanied on the

Cape Town train from Pretoria. The responsibility weighed heavily on my eleven-year-old shoulders to keep us safe overnight and not miss our Makwassie stop in the wee hours of early morning.

Gert and Nienie's son William and his wife, Tienie, lived on a farm nearby and always welcomed me with open arms. For a few weeks each year, surrounded by "family," I could exhale. My passion for cooking originated in Tienie's farm kitchen. Food was prepared daily on a large scale, and eating was big business. I first discovered there the sweet taste of sucking marrow from sheep neck bones. Unlike spring lamb, mutton, the mature sheep, is far more pungent. It became my annual homecoming meal—braised mutton neck with sides of caramelized butternut squash, rice, and potatoes. My other "Tienie" treats included her legendary wild guinea fowl pie and the quintessential South African dessert—milk tart—a rich, creamy vanilla custard in a very light crust dusted with cinnamon.

Tienie frequently took me to the local general dealer to buy much-needed clothes and shoes. She also taught me to sew and rescued many of my near-fatal projects into wearable fashion. I attended a wedding celebration during one of my vacations and Tienie sewed a stunning red dress with tiny colorful flowers scattered over the material for me to wear. The hem and sleeves were trimmed in fine lace. We rolled my long hair in several pieces of pantyhose the night before. I had the most gorgeous locks cascading from a high ponytail and felt so pretty and cherished.

Gert was always present. He was missing a couple of fingers from a mining accident but never let that stop him from creating the most amazing handmade pottery animals. Large and small, they graced his garden and were also scattered across the yard on the farm. He liked flicking me with the fingers he had left whenever he thought I needed a little course correction. I was mesmerized by his medals and stories of serving as an aviation mechanic in North Africa and Italy during WWII.

I kept a selection of his favorite English poems that he eagerly recited to anybody within earshot. The pages were flimsy with age and the author was unknown. Gert had found the poems on postcards in the early 1920s when he was a teenager. He retyped them shortly before he died as a present to me. My online research while writing this memoir led to the discovery that one was a poem called "Thora" by Frederic Edward Weatherly written in 1900. I wished I could tell Gert about the poet who created his treasured words.

Gert was already in his fifties when I was born, and the familiar stoop of age in his shoulders endeared him to me. He was like the wind on my cheeks—just there. We never talked about love. It was as if it was not relevant. The wind doesn't need affirmations that you feel its presence. In return it shows its affection by softly caressing your face and hair with its existence. Maybe that is why I'm so fond of sailing. Initially it was so hard to decipher the direction of the wind and adjust my sail's course to coincide with where I wanted to go. I learned to sail in my early forties and had such difficulty reading the essence of the wind based on the ripples on the water, the feel on my face, and how it lifted the sails to clue me in. When I had to sail my "man overboard maneuvers" for my sailing certification, I think Gert was at the helm steering me.

Nienie was a formidable woman both in size and stature. She was perfectly groomed and coiffed when she presented herself each day. Every morning Gert skillfully managed the many hooks ensuring the proper closure of her oversized corset and thigh-length girdle. Regardless of the occasion, she was permanently clad in pantyhose, sensible pumps, pearls, and painted nails. She did not own casual clothes or sandals, nor did slacks or shorts ever grace her legs. Sitting outside under the African sun in the height of summer would bring most people down, but Nienie never broke a sweat! She took great pride in being a real housewife. Her daily home cooked meals were never burnt. She did the laundry and cleaned her house every day. Today I dedicate my own gleaming clean sink in her honor. She reserved a special sneer for Kitty, aka Mother, whenever her name came up in conversation. Salt of the earth, Nienie took care of me when no one else would.

William was in his final year of high school when I went to live with his parents. Thirteen years separated us. As an only son with middle-aged parents, he enjoyed having me around. He accepted me as a half-sister from the start. While visiting the farm in later years, I would ride alongside him on the tractors, feed the baby chicks and lambs, milk the odd cow, and play with the piglets. We talked about the weather frequently, and I always hesitated to ask if it had rained enough, too much, or if it should be raining soon. I learned there was never a right answer. No doubt, farming and depending on nature's whim of when to rain were not in my career cards.

We often spent the days before and after Christmas with Tienie's parents, who had a very large farm in the area. The size of her extended family was not for the fainthearted. Santa, or Father Christmas in South Africa, always came on Christmas Eve with his bag filled with presents to be distributed by name. Part of me recognized it was really William dressed up in red with a beard.

But the other part had enough faith in the magic of the season to think that Santa would bring my heart's desire. Makwassie awakened potent feelings of wanting to belong. My longing to fit in grew like William's sunflowers, corn, and peanuts when the rain was plentiful. But not too much. For a few weeks each year I was just a happy kid having fun. I never shared with anybody what was happening back in Pretoria. My shame adored being my dirty little secret. I'm sure they suspected trouble because they knew Mother well, but we all pretended everything was hunky-dory.

Comfort Food

WHAT IS IT ABOUT food that I worship so much? Oh, how can I resist its intoxicating spells, smells, and tastes? What is there not to savor when its multitude of textures explode on your tongue? The sweet, the sour, the spicy, the tangy, layered, hidden, exposed . . . its rich flavors are so sensual, satisfying, and sensory. But its real lure lies within its power to transport me to an instant captured from the past. Sometimes my yearning for South Africa leaves me wistful and tinged with melancholy. In Afrikaans, the word is *heimwee*. You can feel the sadness in that long "*ee*." On nights when the longing is particularly overpowering, food spans the divide back to my homeland. My dish of choice is *bobotie*. Slaves from Indonesia and Java brought the spices to Cape Town with them long ago. The complex layer of flavors makes this dish exceptional. Over the years I have added my own twists and turns to a version that reflects my style and taste. It is a delightful concoction of spices, dried fruit, ground beef, and custard—imagine shepherd's pie meeting quiche with curry and garam masala.

After years of risk-taking in the kitchen, these days I seldom bother with a recipe. The fun lies in the experimentation and making of something different. Hand me a basket of your most favorite ingredients. If we are both lucky, it might become a feast or else a fast call for pizza delivery! I show my friends and family the countless layers of my affection through the dishes I create when we can dine together. All I ask in return is to indulge my whimsy for white tablecloths, a candlelit dining room, fine crystal, and some storytelling. Humor me, even if the story has been shared before. Just smile and nod when you hear again how each plate, placemat, napkin, and ring traversed continents to join us at the table. Our dinner plates were made by Pablo Seminario, the Peruvian potter who captures the psyche of the Inca in his work. The hand-embroidered silk placemats found me in India, and our delicate lace napkins came from little villages in Andalucía, Spain. My napkin ring sets were either hand-beaded by Ndebele African women or forged by silversmiths in Cambodia.

On *bobotie* nights we must use rings from my collection of carved African bush animals. You can select yours, but I always pick the leopard. As the most elusive predator and an opportunistic hunter, I feel a kinship with its will to survive alone. I once locked eyes with one during a night drive while on safari. Through the ripples of its muscles and the gold of its startling green eyes, I sensed the sheer power held within its being. It gives me comfort that not everybody requires a group.

When I started high school, the older kids in boarding school forced us younger ones to eat things we didn't like as a form of hazing. We had to "clear" our plates at each meal, and to this day I get chills when presented with sunny-side up eggs. Ugh! I shudder when the yolk runs all over my plate and soaks the rest of the food in slimy yellow. I also avoid liver like a deadly virus and still wince at the memory of its steely taste and the greenish-blue hue of those breakfast liver cakes. Oh, and let's not overlook Beef Tongue Wednesdays! Double ugh! The rubbery, round, multicolored circles floating in creamy mustard sauce reminded me of tree rings.

But there were other pluses. How does one become infatuated with opera? Painfully slowly, perhaps? I was fourteen, stuck at night in study hall at my all-girls' boarding school and grabbed any excuse to be anywhere else. The State Theatre in Pretoria routinely gave the school free tickets to the opera. My first opera was Bellini's *Norma*, certainly not a gentle introduction to the genre. Many nights and four years later, opera joined the ranks of my comfort food. Today when I listen to Maria Callas singing "Casta Diva," the aria from *Norma*, I also yearn for peace. "Nessun Dorma" from *Turandot*, made famous by Pavarotti, is my favorite. The one I know by memory—it nearly gives me the courage to sing it out loud. Luckily for everybody within earshot, I have never moved beyond "nearly"!

Just before my sixteenth birthday, I told Mother that I wouldn't be back to continue practicing sleeping with scissors. I would either stay at boarding school or go home with a schoolmate every weekend and holiday from then on. Calling my bluff, it took a few months for her to realize I was serious. Curiously, she left the Creep and moved into a small apartment in Pretoria. Sleeping on her couch in that flat became my home on the weekends and school holidays. I never understood her motivation for leaving him. Our fights intensified as

I was apparently also responsible for her marriage failing. By then I didn't hold back my own anger. Wow. I really shudder to think what the neighbors thought of our screaming tirades.

Without a husband, her receptionist's salary could not afford a teenage daughter, and I quickly found weekend waitressing jobs. I pulled double shifts and also had a late-night bartending gig at a local nightclub. Although under-aged, nobody checked my birth date and I was paid cash. The best part was that my pay was tied to my sales, and I quickly learned how to upsell. Appetizers, extra sides, desserts, after dinner drinks . . . bingo! The higher the check, the higher my tip and the more I made in sales commission. I discovered the art of persuasion and my initial taste of financial independence. I felt more in control of my fate and grasped that I could survive even if I had to be completely on my own. I also committed the fatal mistake to give Mother money regularly, and it soon became expected.

In addition to my ever-expanding chapters of shame and unworthiness, I was also initiated into the futile art of trying to change people. Mother and I had a honeymoon period shortly after her separation from the Creep. She had never obtained her high school diploma. I offered to help her finish it, as I was studying the same content for my own high school graduation. I was desperately seeking a connection with her, and shared academics seemed like a great opportunity. There was a side benefit, as I imagined her rising to become the person I looked for her to be. One I would be proud to call my mother. The effort ultimately failed. It took several more decades before I scored above a solid "F" on the "accept people as is" exam. I approached fifty years (maybe the wrinkles and grey hair helped) before I was wise enough not to start my sentences with "If only..."

Like some of my failed kitchen attempts, I had to toss my ambition of a healthy mother-daughter relationship in the trash. In high school I turned down a marriage proposal and the chance to drop out as she had at sixteen. She called me crazy for doing so and accused me of throwing my future happiness away for the sake of an education. He was four years older, my first boyfriend, and didn't take my rejection well. Years later our paths crossed briefly, courtesy of the ever-present internet. I learned that he had built a hugely successful business empire and sold it for a large sum of money to an American corporation. I cannot help but think I should have earned a small commission as the initial inspiration to his success!

In the Presence of Greatness

WHO WAS MY FATHER? You know. The guy you slept with who caused me to be born about nine months later. The one you were not married to at the time. The one whose name is NOT on my birth certificate. This mystery man you always dangled in front of me—your bargaining chip for my affection. That man's identity you knew I would crawl through dirt for—my father whom I didn't know. Worse yet. My father who has remained nameless because of your twisted mind. And then you dare want me to call you my mother! And ask me to love you. Wow. Woman, you have balls.

When I was younger and before our relationship took on the foul odor of boiling tripe, Mother would often tell me how proud she was of me. How I was her "only success story." I became curious as to why I didn't share any physical resemblance with her other children. As I got older I pressed her for answers. Instead of denying that I had another father, she fueled the fire. She dropped vague hints regarding someone other than the man she was married to in 1966 being my dad. My all-consuming hunger regarding the truth about my conception gave her such power.

It handed to her the leverage she sought to disarm me with. It was her dirty blunt knife that she could use to make me beg. And oh did she use it! She triggered a fury I could not control. After years of keeping my emotions on a tight rein, my rage against her became primal. I was disgusted to think I carried any of her DNA.

Our days became earmarked by who could hurt the other more. Her elaborate lies about this man sent me on several wild goose chases—only to wind up at dead ends, my wounds raw and bleeding at my core. By now I was a young adult and a computer science student at the University of Pretoria. Initially I aspired to study law, as I wanted to fight injustice and for people not able to defend themselves. But law students were common in South Africa with few scholarship opportunities. I had to adjust my career goals to match what study aid was available. Total Oil, a French multinational oil and gas company, offered me a scholarship in computer science as well as a guaranteed job as a programmer upon graduation. How I disliked its logical and unemotional decision trees, flow diagrams, and instruction code. I didn't know it, but programming would hold my future ticket to America!

Confessions of a burnt-out twenty-year-old: After years of being an exemplary student, I quit bothering. I passed my courses but was seldom in class and rarely found on campus. I had a knack for absorbing large quantities of information in a short time and could recall it for long enough to pass an exam. The carefree days of being a student were lost on me. I was old and tired and didn't see the point in continuing to pretend that I related to my fellow students. I worked in local restaurants seven days a week and made enough money to support a simple lifestyle, a small flat near campus, a scooter, and a horse.

During my second year at university I had started horse riding lessons and was a natural at the sport. Initially I rode the school horses but soon imagined show jumping and dressage competition. My trainer owned a superb black thoroughbred stallion named Caston. He had failed to live up to his bloodline potential at the racetrack and had little value. I adored this creature! Wanting him off his hands, my trainer resold him to me for about $200. His stabling fees proved much higher than my own upkeep and for months I went without so I could afford to keep him. On many a moonlit night Caston and I would fly around a deserted oval-shaped racetrack near the stables. My guardian angels worked overtime keeping my five-foot-four-inch frame from falling and being crushed under his powerful hooves. While grooming him one day, Caston suddenly turned and bit me on my shoulder, although I like to think that he just wanted to show his affection.

On my darkest days Caston was my solace. I spent hours riding him and baring my soul out loud. I sobbed in his mane and allowed my tears to wash away some of the poison blended into my being. My lasting habit to feel connected to nature and all its magnificence was born there. I discovered how, in the face of such purity, I felt whole. When we were in the jumping arena, I marveled at the sheer strength of feeling his force lift me over the obstacles. He was my Pegasus, and I briefly imagined I could fly out of the horrible nightmare I was lost in. The white stripe on his ebony forehead was a beam of light constantly reminding me that I could be guided out of my abyss. He epitomized "The Horse" by Ronald Duncan:

Where in this wide world can man find nobility without pride, friendship without envy, or beauty without vanity?
Here where grace is laced with muscle and strength by gentleness confined.

I had to sell Caston shortly after I graduated from university, as I had no time to continue spending many hours weekly at the stables with him. He was a racehorse and did not thrive with my lack of attention. The sale was conditional on him no longer being a stallion. It was heartbreaking to be the one to change his nature, but the family had small kids and a nice farm. He would be cared for and live in comfort for the rest of his days. It was his white picket fence existence I could give him. At the expense of his balls. Looking back, I now understand that they were more essential and owe him a profound apology. He left immediately following the surgery. To me he will always be the fierce and spirited animal that voluntarily accepted my reins to be on the bit calmly and relaxed. He allowed me to dream it was possible to yield without compromising the essence of self.

Recently I was in Murano, the glass-blowing capital of Italy, and found a reared stallion immortalized in 24-carat gold-plated glass created by a skillful artist. It was as if Caston's fiery attitude was caught within its translucent muscles. The cost of owning such a work of art was irrelevant. I carefully carried the glass stallion across the Atlantic to Dallas and have admired it since. Each day when I see Caston's faded teeth marks on my shoulder, I'm reminded of the many joyful hours I spent with him.

Although I'm no "New Age hippie," my totem is an untethered horse galloping free across wide-open spaces. As a Chinese Fire Horse, I'm fond of the definition from the wonderful world wide web, courtesy of ChinaBuddhismEncyclopedia.com: "Fire Horses are formed from the heat of flames and the wildness of horses, making them as dangerous as they are strong-willed. They fight and kick against boundaries, disregarding traditions, valuing often blind faith over wisdom. The Fire Horse is destined for extremes and adventure and test ordinary men with their bold natures and the heat in their blood. It is futile to try to restrain the will of a Fire Horse as she races through life, chasing the freedom, joy, passion, and independence that feed her." Okay, maybe I'm slightly weird!

Growing up as a white Afrikaans girl in a conservative setting during apartheid also meant that I was raised in a very religious environment. Notwithstanding Mother's warped devotion for all things Jesus, I actively participated in the church adjacent to my high school. The boarding school made it compulsory to attend church twice on Sundays. We wore the most god-awful, hideous, aquamarine Amish-style dresses with white hats that looked like upside-down Dutch ovens. Let me do a simple math calculation of the average number of Sundays over five years that I attended church. I wore that dress and hat more than a thousand times! Like liver cakes and runny eggs, hats are also banned from gracing my head ever again! Except for a running cap and the odd cowboy hat. In addition to our required Sunday attendances, I also taught Sunday school to the younger kids and participated in a midweek youth prayer group.

The late Eighties in South Africa were marked by increased violence against the apartheid regime. The government tried hard to control its white supremacy, including declaring a state of emergency. Among the Afrikaners it was popular to use the Bible to justify treating blacks as a substandard and unequal race.

After years of practicing Christian dogma, my final break occurred one Sunday night in 1986. I attended an evening service with a group of university friends. Our church was very near campus and on Sunday nights it was filled with hundreds of students. I was already fed up with the never-ending scripture lessons from Mother about how I would be on the first-class transport to hell. Our minister dedicated his sermon to apartheid that night. His message was aimed to prove how it was all good with God to practice racial segregation and discrimination. Midway through, more than half of the audience stood up and walked out, me included. I was done with organized faith.

Today my cathedral exists on mountaintops, under desert night skies, and in the ebb and flow of the endless melody of the ocean. I find my God in a fiery sunrise or sunset across the expanse of the horizon where blue meets blue. The sun-kissed summit at dawn or dusk is unrivaled in its ability to impress on me the holiness of being alive. The exquisiteness that nature bestows on me allows me to embrace the majesty of God and creation. It's in that space where I can hear my thoughts and find comfort in my own heartbeat. I can be silent. Daily, in the light of these moments, my everyday struggles are insignificant.

Emerging from My Chrysalis

For all of Mother's overt flaws, mine were subtler. I didn't really know how to love. The unconditional affection naturally existing between a parent and child skipped me. My window to learn to love her closed. Without the wisdom that maturity and understanding brought, I lacked the acumen on how to transform our relationship. My contempt for the decisions she made was large, and rejecting her as "Mother" became the glue that kept me together.

I became a permanent student of how to love. To this day I still struggle with the mystery of what true romantic and intimate connection looks like. The collage I built of my ideal father identity was part Disney fantasy prince mixed with Rambo heroics and blended with the sci-fi know-how of Star Trek's captains Kirk and Picard aboard the *USS Enterprise*. In the absence of any consistent and healthy male influence, I was set up to fail miserably in my search to find a real committed relationship one day. The fragments I pasted together to assemble my dad was a Pablo Picasso version of a deconstructed male. It had little resemblance to any reality.

After running out of fantasy father figures with which to tempt me, Mother's next round of winning my affection reached new lows. In Texas they would have branded her "two-sandwiches-shy-of-a-picnic" crazy. Just before I turned twenty in 1985, she played the "stomach cancer and three months to live" game. I rushed to her side, willing to mend and reconcile our stormy past. Mysteriously, in the absence of any treatment and medication, shortly afterward she made a miraculous recovery. It was the start of how I came to despise all forms of deception. It astounded me to discover that I had any part of me left that could still feel betrayed by her cruel manipulation and lies.

Next, her many empty threats to shoot herself led me to fire back with my own cruel comebacks. "Please make sure you don't miss." "Are you short on money to buy the gun?" "Stick to the bathroom so it's easy to clean up." We were locked in hand-to-hand combat as I spiraled with her into a place that surpassed shame. I wanted to destroy her as much as she wanted to break me. She was slowly winning the game, because until she told me who my father was I could not end the fight.

During this time I met Simone at the San Francisco Steakhouse restaurant near campus where we both worked. We wore black pants, and our blue-and-yellow shirts were cheap imitations of an American football jersey. Nobody there understood that the San Francisco 49ers wore red and gold! Heck, I doubt anybody in South Africa in 1985 knew anything about American football. I certainly never imagined then that one day I would call the US home and root for the Dallas Cowboys! At twenty-three, Simone was four years older than me. South African–born, she'd spent her teenage years growing up in Spain. We could have met at Douglas Adams' "The Restaurant at the End of the Universe," as we came from two galaxies far apart. We sealed our enduring friendship one afternoon after our shift. On the floor in the ladies' bathroom—side by side, holding each other up because we were unable to stand after a feast of prawns and too much wine!

I was charmed by her worldly sophistication and glamorous

international upbringing. I felt a little like Cinderella having stumbled onto her fairy godmother. Simone held the keys to rebuilding me into a sparkling version. The variety that did not include the ugly backstreet fighter I had become. She was fluent in Spanish and had taught English while living in Spain. In my desperate desire to morph into someone I liked, I wanted to learn to speak English well. My limited Afrikaans-laced attempts branded me as naive and inexperienced. Gaining fluency in English would be a powerful way to build a wall between Mother's realm and mine.

Having studied Latin, French, and German in high school, I already had a natural ear for languages. With Simone's continuous tutoring over four years, when I later arrived in the United States I even credited myself as a native English speaker. If it were not for the pesky science and math terminology I stumbled over, perhaps I would never have been found out!

Simone and I became fast friends. Outside of my adopted family in Makwassie, she was the only one who met Mother and spent any time with her. During my last two years at the University of Pretoria we lived next to each other and were inseparable. My duality was never more present. I seamlessly shifted between my new shiny self and the Halloween sequel to Scissors Girl who was warring with Mother. Simone and I had great fun together. I was relieved to let someone into my secret rooms and show her my torture. Thirty years in the making, we are still friends today. She has the honor of being the one person who has known almost all the different phases of "Henda." Like my Makwassie family, we are not defined by blood. Instead we simply choose to love each other wholeheartedly for who we are.

I could listen to her stories about residing abroad for hours. It fueled my own visions of travel. Paris, Madrid, London, Amsterdam, Rome, Barcelona . . . how I hungered to breathe their air and to discover their treasures! Very broke with plenty of student debt, backpacking was the only option I had to explore the Old World.

But I had an obligation to start working for Total Oil in January upon my graduation in 1988. In South Africa the school year runs from January to November. What a revelation when I discovered that Total Oil did not accept mid-year grads. Ah-ha! Therefore failing a minor class in November delayed my graduation by six months. Brilliant bloody idea, even if I had to say so myself. I would not have to report to 9–5 duty at Total Oil until the following January! I didn't have to attend class fulltime to obtain the missing credit either. Saving money for an extended absence was paramount. I found a six-month contract job as an administrative assistant and continued working in restaurants. It was my first taste in disobeying conformity and the rules. I was hooked.

Mother was less enthused with my plans. In her mind I was running away and leaving her with all my student debt and loans. She sent a letter to the University of Pretoria giving them a "heads-up" that I planned to skip town and she refused to be responsible. Nice. She co-signed for my loans as I was under-aged and she was still my legal guardian then. For the record: I paid back every dime anybody has ever loaned me.

Somebody help me! I had no foggy clue how to pack for six months on the road. In a backpack. I borrowed one from a friend and can honestly say I never appreciated that a backpack had so many little side compartments. I wasn't trekking through Europe without a little black dress and strappy sandals . . . just saying! With my priorities straight, after black and strappy I had hardly enough room to squeeze in two extra pairs of jeans, a few T-shirts, one sweater, and a rain jacket.

My money barely stretched to buy a round-trip ticket to Europe and a Eurail youth pass for three months. Taking a gap year was popular, and several of my university friends told me about short-term nanny jobs in England. I contacted the agency when I arrived in London and was overjoyed to receive a five-week position as a companion to a rich elderly English lady!

All my expenses were paid. My duties included lunches at the local pub and afternoon tea with Harvey's Bristol Cream sherry and great conversation. Ms. Caroline was an accomplished pianist who had performed at the Royal Albert Hall in London in her younger days. We spent many rainy days indoors listening to the music of Beethoven, Mozart, and Brahms. She became my private tutor in the genius of classic music. For that I earned £20 per day and saved every penny to fund the remaining months I crisscrossed Europe by train.

Although by myself, I met many other travelers at youth hostels. Without any plans I often took overnight trains to save the cost of a bed. Back then they allowed us to sleep in the corridors using our backpacks as pillows. I learned how little I needed each day and how much I loved the exploring of unknown places. I felt so untroubled as each day unfolded uniquely original. My lasting passion to uncover the mystery of our planet officially began. The many remarkable cities I had read about showed me their treasures and I discovered my affection for original art and sculpture. I visited all the phenomenal museums across Europe and became friends with Rembrandt, Van

Gogh, Vermeer, Picasso, Monet, Renoir, Goya, Dali, Turner, Rodin, Matisse, Michelangelo, Caravaggio, and so many more. To this day it makes me happy to spend time with the Old Masters in the great cities across the globe. Their exhibits also frequently visit North Texas galleries and I try to rendezvous with them whenever possible.

Close to my Dallas home, I have many favorite pieces scattered between the Nasher Sculpture Garden, the Kimbell Art Museum, the Dallas Museum of Art, and the Modern in Fort Worth. But there is one work that is singularly superior. It is a wooden ladder at the Modern reaching to heaven. The artist is Martin Puryear and he named the piece *Ladder for Booker T. Washington*. Carved from a single ash sapling, the artist used primitive techniques to smooth the bark and split the sapling in two exact halves. I speculated how nervous he must have been as there was no room for error. I like knowing that he was willing to risk failure to create something so extraordinary. He dared greatly.

Butterfly Days

PARIS IN THE FALL . . . priceless and precious! I halted my traversing across Europe to spend a few weeks in the City of Light and Romance while staying with Simone's sister. Her name was Nicole, but she was "Nicky" to those of us who loved her. She lived in a luxury two-bedroom apartment near the Eiffel Tower and worked at the South African embassy.

Finding Paris irresistible was effortless. How can anyone object to its charm? My metro stop was École Militaire and for six weeks

I lived and breathed all things Paris. I could see the Eiffel Tower from my bedroom window and spent many early mornings on the steps of the Sacré Coeur watching day break over the city. I was on a first-name basis with my waiter at our neighborhood brasserie and shopped for bread, meat, and cheese alongside the locals while practicing my school French. At night Nicky showed me the more expensive side of Paris, unaffordable on my backpack budget. We went to the famous Maxim's as well as all her favorite places on the Left Bank. Out of all the great cities, Paris held a unique currency for me, and like a great novel I was captured within its story. Similarly, some of Nicky's glamour brushed off on me. Like Simone, she was the epitome of sophistication, style, and elegance. When I left Paris I felt even more like a polished penny, having learned to successfully hide my dull, worn side.

Still drunk on the euphoria of being a newly minted world traveler, I struggled to conform to working at a real job back in Johannesburg after six months on the road. My tiny cubicle at Total Oil was on the 22nd floor of an all-glass building. Sitting next to the window made me quickly realize that manmade heights frightened me. Put me on the side of a mountain and I'm fine, but my legs freeze walking down a fire escape. My Polish boss also immediately exposed my limited computer programming expertise. Geez. I didn't think I would so quickly be unmasked. I didn't exactly learn much while attending university. To do that I would have had to be in class. I became his punching bag and after a few months I was terrorized by my own ineptness at coding. No doubt my "scholarship" employee status was all that saved me from being fired. The company had to recoup the money they'd invested in my education.

The impasse appeared in the form of a bubble-sort algorithm. It is a simple comparison that repeatedly goes through the items to be sorted, swapping them if they are in the wrong order. Mr. Smarty Pants tasked me with coding a bubble sort, knowing I would fail. He probably reveled at the prospect of another chance to ridicule me in front of my coworkers. It took the entire night but I learned to code with the patience and goodwill of a colleague who helped me. When my boss arrived the next morning, I had a perfectly functioning bubble sort! Liberated from my insecurity, within a few months I was considered an asset. I discovered my fondness for using complex code to write computer programs to do as I commanded. Henda the control freak emerged. Imagine that!

Still, my core craved the freedom I had found on the road. I successfully negotiated an unpaid sabbatical after my first year. Jubilantly I packed my backpack (this time with great proficiency!) and trekked for seven weeks through the Middle East. The trip had a rough start when I discovered upon arrival that Ramadan coincided with my plans. Though not a Muslim, I followed the custom to eat before sunrise or after sunset, as very few eateries were open during the day.

I spent most of my time in Turkey, a country that captured my imagination. Buses transferred me from Istanbul to Ankara, Cappadocia to the Black Sea, then south to the Aegean Sea and the old city of Ephesus. I seldom ran into people who could speak English. To most of the locals at the time, a Western woman by herself wearing jeans was something peculiar and to be avoided. I also stopped in Israel, Cypress, and some of the Greek islands. As a white South African during apartheid, I was unable to include Egypt and

Jordan as we were not allowed entry. I could never have guessed then that one day our paths would cross in a memorable way.

I reluctantly returned to my desk in Johannesburg after I got home, trapped once more in the boredom of writing computer code. I continued to waitress in my spare time to save up for my next adventure. The United States was in my crosshairs, but the dollar was strong, distances far, and the States were not budget friendly for backpackers. By now I had two years left on my contract with Total Oil, and they had received their money's worth. I had seamlessly transformed into a very high-performing star employee.

Mother and I were still in a standoff. In the days before cell phones, she would call me at the office offering a sweet greeting, "Henda, it's Mommy." I would just as sweetly reply, "Hello. Ready yet to tell me who my father is?" The conversation seldom progressed beyond the single click of me hanging up on her after that. I refused to budge from my ultimatum of no further contact unless she told me the truth.

The restaurant where I worked featured a groovy five-piece jazz band on Sunday nights. They always dedicated the song "New York, New York" to me. I was positive that my vagabond shoes would lead me there. I too would wake up in the city that never sleeps, one way or another. Toward the end of 1990 America came calling! I responded to an ad in the local Sunday newspaper for computer programmers. The interview was fifty minutes away on my little scooter. Although dusty and windblown in appearance, I nailed it and the headhunting firm offered me a consulting job in North Carolina. It was time to pack, big time!

Exit Stage Left, 1990

I CAUGHT HER HAND in mid-air. *Don't you dare hit me!* Our final hour. No surprise it came to this. It was twenty-four years in the making and had no happy ending in the script. The week before she had left a letter under my door cursing me. She expressed her hopes for my children to be deformed and retarded one day. Bitch. The reason she showed up at my door with her husband #3 that fateful night is vague and no longer relevant. It was the night I recognized that I was in fourth grade again and had to devise another safety plan. I realized how intense my shame was of the person she could bring out in me—it was the worst version of me and one I no longer wanted to keep. It was the part of me that could destroy me, and it made me recoil how ugly, hateful, and filled with vengeance it was.

A few days before I had already sunk to the bottom. I'd had lunch with the Creep. The one who would have raped me if I'd given him the chance. We dined liked civilized, nice people and made idle conversation about this and that. She had dangled one final father story and hinted that this despicable creature could shed light on the puzzle. Of course he hadn't, and when I left lunch that day I felt worse than a whore. I'd sold a piece of my consciousness in exchange for the knowledge of who had fathered me. Never. Never. Never again, I'd vowed. It was not worth the price.

Let's stop the madness now. She gave birth to me, but I had the will to interrupt the destructive sequence. She had tried to hit me that night because I finally had the courage to tell her to her face that she didn't know whom she had slept with at the time I was created. I left for the United States shortly afterward and promised myself that I would never see her again.

Out of the night that covers me,
Black as the pit from pole to pole,
I thank whatever gods may be
For my unconquerable soul.

In the fell clutch of circumstance
I have not winced nor cried aloud.
Under the bludgeonings of chance
My head is bloody, but unbowed.

Beyond this place of wrath and tears
Looms but the Horror of the shade,
And yet the menace of the years
Finds, and shall find me, unafraid.

It matters not how strait the gait,
How charged with punishments the scroll,
I am the master of my fate:
I am the captain of my soul.

—"INVICTUS," WILLIAM ERNEST HENLEY

Oh Africa, My Africa!

I FELT AN INTENSE urge to touch the giant Leadwood tree in front of me. With a formidable silhouette against the clear African sky, the tree's trunk was massive in diameter. It stood solitary at the intersection of two dirt roads. I was in the Sabi/Lion Sands Game Reserve near Kruger National Park in South Africa on my first visit back since I had left as a young adult.

Teeming with wildlife around us, I realized that getting out of an open Land Rover in the middle of the bush seemed a bit foolish. Especially since we just spotted a large troop of baboons and a leopard on the hunt. The powerful draw of running my hands over the pale grey bark and tracing the deeply cracked rectangular pieces of the trunk was far more compelling than my concern of becoming prey. With the park ranger's blessing and his rifle loaded and ready if necessary, I approached the ancient tree with reverence. Considered by the natives to be the ancestor of man and animal, its fissured facade reminded me of the parched desert sand waiting for rain to ooze into the crevices, bringing brand-new growth.

Larger than life up close, I slowly ran my fingers over the hard wood and allowed its rough exterior, akin to reptilian scales, to softly scuff my skin. Because of its density, it is the only wood to sink in water, and its ash, when mixed with water, can be used as bush toothpaste. Unshed tears stung my eyes, and I used the massive trunk to shield me from my fellow safari-goers watching from our Land Rover. They would not have understood how I'd shunned my bush love when I moved to America. They couldn't know how this desire had forged inside me early on and how it had unconditionally known that I would be back one day.

At age twenty-four I had left South Africa filled with rage about the unfair hand of cards I had drawn growing up in an environment that required me to battle when I should have been allowed to just play. My fury had fumed at the forces that took away my childhood innocence at a tender age. When I should have been just loved unconditionally. I was angry at the unjust years of struggle to redefine my future. With only my own unwavering promise to never allow myself to become another statistic of sad circumstances, I'd left with the burning desire to find a safe harbor. Somewhere I could drop anchor and either heal or hide.

At twenty-seven, three years after arriving fresh from Africa in North Carolina, I was the proud owner of a US Green Card. I no longer had the constraints of being an alien on a work visa. As a permanent resident I finally had the freedom to choose my employer and select wherever I wanted to live in the United States. The Deep South and small-town USA were not long-term matches for me. Having grown up in Pretoria and Johannesburg, I craved the buzz of the big city. I also wanted to live near a large international airport with easy access to foreign destinations and cheap airfare.

By then I was a certified advanced scuba diver and fully addicted to adventures above and below the water. I had used every dime to crisscross the country and the Caribbean. Saving a dollar was not on my agenda! I'd met a man about eight months after my arrival in the US as a business referral. He was a financial planner and had offered his services to help me save money. Instead we started dating the following year.

Coopers & Lybrand, one of the big consulting and accounting firms, offered me a technical consulting position and I jumped at the chance. Together we settled in Dallas in the spring of 1994, partly to be close to my boyfriend's family in Oklahoma City and San Antonio. Mostly because Dallas offered plenty of business opportunities for both of us. On behalf of Coopers & Lybrand I accepted a consulting position at Sprint, the telecommunications company.

The wheels of my reinvented reality were spinning smoothly over the tracks. Job? Check. Guy? Check. House with a swimming pool and a nice car? Check, check. I could have checked off my re-engineered image of "All American Girl Next Door" were it not for the very small matter of my bloody accent that I couldn't shake! I fully embraced being an American, and I foolishly believed that I could keep the little cracks from yesteryear hidden indefinitely.

Yet now, at almost forty years old, standing in front of this tree reaffirmed how vivid my African affection was. It reinforced the truth that despite my revulsion toward my mother, I had secretly kept a small drawer filled with the possibility that one day I could move back home. For years I had draped myself in the comfort of a blanket with stars and stripes on the outside, and a hidden rainbow flag of the new South Africa that I'd left behind on the inside. I would proudly affirm myself an American African to anyone inquiring about my origins. Although I placed my hand across my heart during the Star-Spangled Banner, I had to confess that except for the first and last lines, I didn't really know the words. Granted, I also didn't know the words to "Nkosi Sikelel' iAfrika" (God Bless Africa) except for the few lines in Afrikaans. I guess that made me neither much of an American nor African patriot.

When I ditched the country of my birth I had no intention of ever returning. But here I was, having retraced my steps back to Africa. Sixteen years gone in a snap-crackle-pop. The reason I'd returned was tragic and unexpected. I wanted to tell the Leadwood tree why I was back in Africa—the story about a great woman whom I had called treasured and trusted. One of my fairy godmothers. Instinctively, however, I grasped that they were friends too, and I could just quietly be present. Tears were not required to drive my loss home. Overcome by the sheer phenomenon of a specimen older than many civilizations, I yearned for it to whisper its secrets of endurance. I longed to linger under its whitish branches and let its wisdom saturate my bones. I wanted to tell its ruptured surface of my own splintered secrets that had arisen since I'd left.

Wait. Hang on. I jumped ahead a little. Forgive me my inability to tell you the story in a nicely organized sequential format! Before I tell you any more about my South African homecoming, I have to get married, deliver babies, and put the finishing touches on my fairytale American reality.

Wedding Bells Are Ringing!

WHAT A FANTASTIC AND signature year 1995 was! By my 29th year of breathing air I had so successfully morphed into my American self that I was unaware that South Africa hosted and won the Rugby World Cup.

It was the year I would officially become part of a family, my boyfriend's family. I could finally sever my link to my maiden name, Hendriks. Yeah, really, Henda Hendriks. Shall we talk about the constant cruel teasing I endured in school with silly rhymes making fun of the combination? I had considered officially changing my last name to a version of my middle name when I turned eighteen. I liked the sound of Henda Elayne and thought it was a cool variation on Elaine.

I hated Hendriks. Every time I signed it, said it, and had to claim it, it mocked me with the truth that it wasn't real—a daily reminder that I had no identity. My father was unknown and I didn't have a dad, step or adopted, growing up. Naturally, boys were extraterrestrial creatures. I was a brainy, nerdy overachiever at an all-girls' high school. I had very curly hair, crooked teeth, and a pimpled face and I wore glasses. Oh, and the boarding school didn't allow hairdryers until my senior year. Wow. Thinking back, I really needed a serious makeover. Thank the good Lord I didn't go to a co-ed school, as I'm not sure I could have survived the wounds of such deficits!

Post high school, my dating track record had been dismal. (Note: it was absent before, so "dismal" was an actual improvement.) I could blow dry my hair straight, had invested in contact lenses, and outgrew the zit phase. Thanks to a scooter crash and a capped front tooth, I also had somewhat presentable teeth. Under Simone and Nicole's influence my wardrobe and dress sense had also expanded drastically.

My jaunts around the world had further glossed up my image. In four short years I had become a sophisticated, worldly art and music aficionado who could speak English almost flawlessly. People thought I was northern European—Danish, maybe? In my haste to become a princess overnight I should have taken notes about the midnight clock and pumpkin part of the fairytale.

Nevertheless, I was so singularly focused on my goals to redefine my being that I had no time for men to distract me. I was a virgin well into my early twenties. Prior to leaving South Africa my longest stretch of seeing a man had lasted about six weeks when I'd worked for Total Oil. He was an Israeli entrepreneur who lived in South Africa. We met on the airplane when I flew back from the Middle East after my backpacking excursion. He was probably the most good-looking male specimen I'd ever met, past or present. I'm not sure how well he aged, but certainly back then he could have commanded his very own *David* statue. He ushered me into the age of courtship and skillfully broadened my education in the art of exploration. But not enough to stay in South Africa with him.

Initially when I arrived in North Carolina, I became entangled with a redneck crowd from Vermont. They hung out every night at the local dive bars nearby. I was initiated into drinking cheap beer and jug wine, shooting jello-shots, eating one-topping pizza, watching American sports, and throwing darts while playing pool and shuffleboard. Night after night after night. After months of trying I dumped the mind-numbing efforts to adapt to their existence. For someone who didn't even like beer, I drank enough to last me a few lifetimes!

In contrast, when I met Rick, he had a graduate degree and a successful business. He had traveled to several destinations throughout the world, was well read and sophisticated, and liked great food, music, and wine. And ta da—his dad was a Spaniard! After my first miserable year in the Deep South, spending time with him was akin to vacationing in a lush tropical paradise. It felt as if I was in Hawaii, surrounded by wild orchids and sipping exotic drinks with little umbrellas while reciting poetry. His large extended family spanned continents from Oklahoma City, San Antonio, Peru, and Andalusia, Spain.

He offered me safety and the chance to blend in—something I'd fantasized about since I was a little girl on the farm back in Makwassie. He took me to Oklahoma City our first Christmas together when we were dating. I donned a sweater with little jingle bells sewn on and easily got caught up in the holiday joy of swans and geese, hens, golden rings, and birds in a pear tree.

His dad and I shared the unique bond of being immigrants. We'd both given up our culture, language, and country to mix our identity with our chosen country. I felt linked to his journey, as it had many similarities to my own.

I wanted the classic American dream: 2.5 kids, a house with a manicured lawn, rows of bright and happy seasonal plantings where weeds were pulled weekly. I envisioned us growing old together, sitting side by side in our rocking chairs with our grandkids running around. I was willing to do whatever to make that happen. I would reshape my essence if I could be part of this uncomplicated normal. Certainly I could wipe my blackboard clean. As the master chameleon I never doubted that I could sculpt myself to be a wife and mother without any sharp or uneven edges.

The months leading up to my wedding day were washed in the typical chaos of a bride to be. There were millions of moving parts preparing for the day to feel like an adored and gorgeous princess. My future mother-in-law was an authority at arranging large gatherings, and under her supervision no detail was missed. One day fourteen years later, she would be the one to save my life. Perhaps she is the real reason I became part of the Salmeron tribe at all.

We married on September 3, 1995, in All Saints Catholic Church in Oklahoma City. William escorted me down the aisle, as Gert was too frail to make the journey from Makwassie. My bouquet was a small imitation of Princess Diana's, and my gown was a Jim Hjelm raw silk and lace design that I bought at a resale shop in Dallas for $600.

Simone and Nicole came from South Africa to be my bridesmaids and wore the midnight blue dresses that I'd handpicked to compliment my ivory gown. Standing next to me in front of more than 250 wedding guests, they witnessed our vows. Years later Simone confessed how shocked they were by the person who had picked them up at the airport. I was unrecognizable from the rebellious and nonconforming friend from our early twenties. It was also the last time I ever saw my dearest friend Nicky. How I wish I'd had a small looking glass into the future!

Friday the 13th, June 1995

THREE MONTHS BEFORE MY big day I received a startling phone call at my office in Dallas. A police lieutenant from Pretoria was on the other line. "Are you in danger, ma'am?" he asked.

Apparently Mother had reported me to the South African authorities as having been kidnapped. According to her story I had been missing for several weeks and so a full-blown search for my whereabouts ensued. It had been five years since the familiar madness had surged through my veins. I felt as if I'd been kicked hard in the stomach. For a few moments I couldn't breathe. I was lightheaded and had to swallow the rising bile in my throat. I listened to him explain how the authorities had planned the following week to feature me as a missing person on milk cartons throughout South Africa. These were the days before the reach of social media and Amber Alerts about missing children. I had to credit Mother for a very original concoction. I could never imagine devising such a bizarre lie to anybody, much less the police. I immediately suspected she had been motivated by money and that husband #3 was the real missing person.

Since I had left South Africa in 1990, Mother and I had not maintained any contact. I had blocked out ever having had a mother—so much so that I almost believed my fabricated story that I so easily shared with others about growing up as an orphan. Whenever anyone asked if I had family back in South Africa, it was so much easier to deny claims to any and declare that I had grown up as a ward of the state. To say that I had "family" back home would have validated my upbringing as normal, and I certainly had no plans to confess the truth to strangers.

Trying to remain calm, I explained to the lieutenant on the phone that I was neither lost nor abducted. As a legal resident of the United States, I added, I would report him for harassment if he ever contacted me again. I smiled slightly at my empty threats and speculated what kind of response I would have received from the United States government. The officer then gave me Mother's mailing address and pleaded with me to reach out to her. I felt sorry for him, as I was sure that he was a good man just doing his job and hoping to close the file.

Suddenly my carefully constructed bandages were ripped off, leaving my old wounds freshly bleeding. As I hung up the phone I finally voiced the words I'd never said out loud: *I hate my mother.* A few weeks later, using a friend's return address in New York City, I sent her a letter absent of all pleasantries and left unsigned. It held a single phrase in Afrikaans: *Who is my father?*

Shortly before my wedding I received her response. It took a long time before I had the courage to read what was hidden inside. No part of me ever wanted to set foot on South African soil again. I never wanted to go back to be reminded of the monster I'd allowed her to turn me into. I realized I was still gripping the scissors beyond those nights when I could have been physically hurt. The full force of my anger terrified me, and all I could do was stuff it into a very dark corner in the farthest regions of my psyche. I pretended that it didn't matter and I didn't care.

Building with Blocks

AFTER OUR HONEYMOON IN Taos and Santa Fe, we settled comfortably into a Dallas routine. By the spring of 1999 I was a senior technical expert for what was now PricewaterhouseCoopers when Sprint offered me a full-time position with them. It was tempting as it came with the ultimate golden handcuffs: the opportunity to telecommute from my home near White Rock Lake in Dallas. With a newborn son I decided it was impossible not to accept. My daughter was born two years later, and I happily performed my job with a baby on my lap and a toddler playing nearby under the watchful eyes of a fulltime nanny.

We traveled often, including vacations to Europe and Spain to visit the extended Salmeron family. As a couple, we were actively involved in our neighborhood and enjoyed volunteering for many good causes. I was well established in my career, earned a good income, and seemed to have reached the perfect American narrative I craved. I had very little contact with any of my South African friends, and the recollections from my tumultuous past faded into a gentle tone of sepia.

My life's engine ran on an easy beat, and a happy ending looked promising. Oops—not so fast. In the aftermath of September 11, 2001, the tech bubble crashed hard. I considered myself a good corporate employee and my company position was not at risk. But many of my colleagues were not so lucky. Their layoffs became my first lesson in how disposable a workforce can be. The regime hired in the wake to clean house promptly terminated the telecommuting policy. Like naughty children we were summoned back to the office, only to spend every day on conference calls in cubicles since all of our customers were in other states.

These lessons awakened in me the overpowering ambition to work for myself. Overnight, my American entrepreneurial spirit was lit. I decided to leave corporate America and become a real estate agent. A little drastic you say? It was nuts! I had just given up a very cushy and high-paying corporate job for the great unknown of commission real estate sales. How did I celebrate the 2003 Martin Luther King holiday in mid-January? Unemployed, with a severe panic attack!

You may be curious what flow chart brought me to my latest crazy. Leading up to resigning, I'd studied my local Dallas real estate market thoroughly. I felt I could draw on my many years of corporate and business experience to run a successful real estate practice. And I came "geek" strong. Technology was my buddy! We spoke HTML code. I felt confident that I could succeed in a field where many agents were part time, lacked computer competence, and frankly were not very professional.

The scrappy teenager from the Eighties living off waitress sales commission collided with the thirty-something living off real estate commission. Neither had the safety net of a base salary. Once again it was feast or famine! Hard work had also been my companion since I was little. The frequent fifteen-hour days, seven-day workweeks that mark residential real estate has never fazed me. In exchange I fancied the freedom of being my own boss. Work or play? Work or vacation? Work or relax? Why choose one over the other? Both blended together and I learned to shape-shift easily between the two, sometimes simultaneously.

My enjoyment for what I do stretches far beyond a commission check or the liberty of sleeping in on a weekday. It makes me happy to help people. Uncertainty and transition are scary places I know well. I grasp how hard it is to start over in a new place when you don't know anybody. I don't sell bricks and mortar. Instead I'm your partner and guide to find a place you can call home. I'm honored when you hand me your front door keys and let me into your private spaces. It's not relevant to me whether it's a multimillion-dollar estate or a starter home. The one only has a few more zeroes. What matters is the same. I want to do the best I can. All I can offer you is my guidance, wisdom, and expertise. Oh, and by the way, being an expert at transformation I do one helluva job converting houses from messy, lived-in everyday disasters to beautiful and elegant staged swans floating down the real estate river. I should consider writing that real estate memoir!

The unexpected rewards of my career had nothing to do with money. Many of my clients became my closest and most cherished friends. Their presence added immense value I had never planned on when I embarked on this endeavor. For that I'm sincerely grateful.

A few weeks after my big initial freak-out, my very first public open house occurred during one of those rare snow days in Dallas. I plodded through several inches of icy slush in high heels to post signs directing potential buyers to the house. Although it took several months before we finally found the house of their dreams, I met my first buyer clients that winter's day, a mother and her daughter. As it would so often, my marvelous universe placed its own direction signs for me to follow. I could not have foreseen the role that my first buyers would play years later at a pivotal intersection on my path.

South African Homecoming

I WILL NEVER HAVE the right words. I've tried for years to herd them into a proper sentence, but stubbornly they are still willful and wild in my heart. How do I tell you about this sorrow and loss? It was my introduction as to why clichés exist. All we have is here and now. Carpe diem. Tomorrow may never come. You only live once. Yup. All true. But they took on a distinct meaning when Simone called a few days before Christmas in 2005. We had not spoken in a few years, having last seen each other the night I got married ten years earlier. Her message was tragically simple. Nicky was dead. So young. Such an awful accident.

I had run out of time to tell Nicky, "I love you." The vehement loathing for my mother had poisoned everything about South Africa. In its nasty wake I chose to neglect all the people who were important to me. Gert. Nienie. William. Tienie. Simone. Nicole. My high school friends. My university friends. My Total Oil work friends. Everybody. Bitterly misguided, I had turned my back and walked away from all of them. Let's be honest. I cannot blame the clichés for uniting to shake me around and get my attention. But a kinder, earlier warning from them would have been nice, as I also never saw Gert or Nienie alive again.

It had been more than thirteen years since I'd last gazed at an African sunrise or sunset when Nicky's untimely death and memorial led me back home. Like on a premature salmon run, I returned to the place of my birth. How surprising to discover that within my newfound American heart, my African blood still flowed unchecked.

While there I found myself initially wishing more than once to be able to live there and reclaim some of the missing years. I was intoxicated again with the exquisite African light and the way my soul was quiet and at peace when the African bush surrounded me. I realized how much I had missed my people and my culture and—above all—its earth, mountains, and oceans whose moods, smells, and sounds brought such familiar pleasure.

But I had an American family now. My years on US soil had steadily mounted. I was proud of my American Way that I had built from scratch with my bare hands. Looking down on the continent as the plane carried me back to Dallas, I concluded I simply had to visit often. I promised to bring my kids soon. I wanted Africa to crawl under their skin, into their being, and let them be enchanted by its seduction. Half of their roots originated from its shores and although my part of their family tree was sparse, I no longer deemed it a disgrace.

I was American with just enough African spice to be different. One day I would like one-third of my ashes to be placed inside the Leadwood giant in the Sabi/Lion Sands Game Reserve. I like the thought of spending a few thousand years sharing stories with my old bush friend and letting its hardwood protect me from the elements. I take great comfort in the old Zulu saying, "There is no spirit that does not come home." Mine just had to wander while getting lost a few times.

Before leaving South Africa, I tucked a wallet-sized picture of Nicky in my purse. I have carried it with me since. Her daily presence is my everyday reminder to be mindful of time. My frequent silent conversations with her include my gratitude for her priceless gift: to freely own the South African within, without yesterday's hurt.

She initiated the sinkhole and ultimate collapse of the fictitious "Henda." Mourning her was the unearthing of my own authenticity without shame. My mother was living in Pretoria when I returned for Nicky's memorial. I chose not to look her up. I'd already closed her book permanently after I read her letter to me about my father. But it would take almost a decade longer before I could fully end the emotional reign my mother had over me.

Augury in Pink, Late Summer 2008

DUSK ANNOUNCED ITS ARRIVAL and so did the super moon as it crept out from the shadows. The sky was a spectacular showcase of crimson strips on an azure canvas. The scattered marshmallow clouds were shaped like antelopes, giraffes, and other plains game on the African savanna. Texas may fall short of mountain marvels and ocean poetry, but the vastness of a Texas sky never fails to astonish me. After dusk departed, the stars shone like lavish stones in a crown fit for royalty.

My teenage son and I had come to the drive-in movie theater in Ennis about thirty miles from downtown Dallas. I'd wanted to dislodge old memories of going to the drive-in as a child. Back then we hung the crackly speaker off the car window and watched a movie on a big screen under an even bigger sky. My German sedan with the South African flag bumper sticker seemed conspicuous amid the pick-ups and SUVs in this small Texas town. My South African accent while buying our tickets didn't help me much either! I was marked an alien and I briefly wished I could speak "Ennis." But the effort proved well worth it when minutes later I snuggled under a blanket with Mateo on my car hood, leaning against our pillows.

Watching an outdoor movie was a welcome reprieve from the stress from earlier that day. A few days before, I'd received a call from the mother I'd met at my very first open house many years earlier. She sought my help selling the home they'd purchased from me. I was completely caught off guard to learn that part of why she had called me was to tell me that her daughter had a Stage 4 cancer diagnosis. She had little time left because her breast cancer had metastasized into advanced bone cancer. That afternoon I found myself sitting in their family room, hugging the daughter in my arms and trying hard to hold back my tears. She was barely older than I was and had simply run out of time to marry and have children.

Without words to comfort her, I felt powerless in the face of its injustice and cruelty. It was my first brush with terminal breast cancer. I couldn't foresee then how the color pink would become such an intimate part of my own future.

The Messenger

WHAT IS ON YOUR bucket list? You know. Those things we want to do before our time is up. Mine is much longer than my daily to-do list. I fancy winning the lottery so I can tick each one of them off: Summit Kilimanjaro. Trek the Australian Outback. Set foot on Antarctica. Dance the salsa in Cali, Colombia. Watch the polar bears in Churchill, Manitoba. Scuba Kona and Hawaii's famed Manta Ray night dive. Hike across Iceland. Take the train from Moscow to Vladivostok. Ride with the great wildebeest migration from the Serengeti to the Maasai Mara—on horseback! Munch on street food in Marrakesh, Morocco. Scuba dive the annual sardine run in Durban, South Africa. Billions of sardines move northward from the cold Agulhas Bank near Cape Town toward Mozambique. During this ocean spectacle thousands of dolphins chase the sardines and drive them into tight circles. It becomes the frenzied feeding ground of predators including sharks, whales, game fish, birds, and seals. I want to see it! Sigh. This is just the tip of my list for exploring and experiencing earth's bounty before my hourglass is empty.

In early May 2009 I was fortunate to dive in Placencia, Belize. It was during the annual spring migration of the whale sharks—another dive I wanted to check off. I was warned about it being challenging because some divers sense extreme disorientation. The dive occurs in bottomless blue open water in the absence of reefs, walls, or the ocean floor for guidance. I was uncertain how I would react and shared my unease with the dive master just before splashing overboard. He stayed close by, holding eye contact as we descended.

As suspected, I had an immediate claustrophobic feeling because I lost my reference point and felt as if I was drowning in cobalt. Freaked out, I briefly contemplated aborting the dive when the dive master left my side to assist another panicked diver in the group.

I coerced myself to just breathe as I slowly relaxed and surrendered to the richest sapphire I had ever seen. The concentrated blue was dotted with millions of white specks of plankton that gave me the feeling of floating among the stars in space. Our descent continued to approximately 100 feet. The ocean extended more than 3,300 feet beneath us where thousands upon thousands of Cubera snapper spawned. The whale sharks came to Placencia during the spring to feast on these snapper spawn as well as other small fish and plankton. The gentle giants were filter feeders and totally docile beasts. Almost the size of school buses, they were also intimidating. Like all things untamed, we were warned there was no guarantee that we would spot any during our estimated 45-minute dive.

From the depths beneath me, an enormous shadow suddenly appeared. "Whale shark!" I futilely shouted aloud through my regulator as the animal came closer. Prior to the dive we were also cautioned about stiff fines if we tried to approach or touch a whale shark. But nobody had explained what to do when a whale shark approached you! Mistaking my fellow divers' air bubbles for spawn, the whale shark tried eating the bubbles from our regulators in a curious and playful way. He weaved through the divers and even nipped at some of their tanks. I took photographs as fast as I could and feverishly hoped that at least one might capture this immense creature.

Suddenly the whale shark turned right toward me! I hung motionless in the water. Luckily my camera was attached to my BC jacket as I dropped it by my side. In seconds he was mere inches away from my face. Staring into his eyes, my thoughts were suspended in the timeless space surrounding us. I slowly raised my hands and lightly ran them over his mouth that was big enough to swallow me. I then gently pushed him to one side, and he glided effortlessly underneath me. As I watched him disappear into the abyss, I had to blink very hard to stop tears from running down my cheeks and fogging my dive mask.

The dive occurred exactly thirty days before I felt a little lump in my right breast in late May. During the next year there would be many times when I would transport myself back to this moment when the whale shark and I locked eyes. I would come to think of him as a messenger sent to give me the courage I would require to run the course. It felt as if I had looked into the eyes of God.

ACT 2
CANCER

Adventurous
Crazy
Beautiful

Wishes to go where people don't just say Merry Christmas
Dreams of changing the world
Wants to explore
Who loves to travel

Who fears cockroaches
Who is afraid of heights
Who likes to run
Who believes in a difference

Who loves Rooibos tea
Who loves to scuba dive
Who loves nature and the outdoors
Who loves South Africa

Who plans to stay successful in life
Who plans to be different
Who loves to laugh
Whose final destination is heaven

My mom, Henda

—DOMINIQUE SALMERON'S FIFTH-GRADE MOTHER'S DAY POEM, 2012

East Texas in Springtime

THE GUINEA FOWLS PLAYED chase through the vineyard. Their dark grey feathers glistened in the sun, and the dense white spots covering their plumage reminded me of the speckled coat of a whale shark. The female's two-syllable call "come-back, come-back" transported me to the farm in Makwassie in South Africa. As I watched them scurry around the vines looking for insects, I appreciated what a delightful way it was to enjoy my Sunday morning at a winery in East Texas.

The breeze gently lifted the young green grapevines, and I could sense the earth's anticipation of the fruit forming within. Row upon row the vines were cuffed to their trellises, training their tender growth to obey how the vintner wanted them to spread. Restricted but free simultaneously, it was a great study of the dichotomy I found within. With a craving to be wild and free, I was also bound to my reality. Cursed with the acute longing to explore the earth far and wide, the day-to-day requirements of existing seemed so restrictive.

I was in Tyler, Texas, to speak at a 2015 breast cancer conference. My layman's topic amid oncologists, radiologists, and breast surgeons? How pink became my badge of hope and courage. Combining the passion of red with the purity of white, pink comes in many shades. My wardrobe today holds an extensive assortment of the many tones of pink, from the lightest blush to a blazing hot pink coat daring a cold winter's day away. As I reflected on how I had come to this point, I was brought back six years earlier to a June morning in 2009.

June 7, 8:35 A.M.: "Henda, I'm so sorry but the biopsy confirmed you have breast cancer. So far the pathology shows it's the most treatable type. It looks like the tumor is small, and we caught it early."

In an instant my forty-two-year-old life was disrupted. While living my Dallas routine I had been oblivious to the time bomb slowly ticking against my breastbone. Pink ribbons and breast cancer happened to other people and older women, and until then it was not part of my reality. I had annual mammograms. In fact, just a few months earlier in December 2008, I'd had my fourth clear one. Like many women, I considered a mammogram foolproof. Although I knew that one in eight women will get the news none of us wants to hear, I had never considered drawing the "C" card.

What would have happened to me had I not decided in early spring 2009 to alter my "over" and "un" course—overweight and overstressed, unfit and unhealthy? After years of working fifteen-hour days it was time to suspend my slide into a few extra pounds and elevated blood pressure. Going to the gym held no appeal, nor did running or any of the usual boring conditioning options. My house was near the shores of White Rock Lake in Dallas and rowing turned out to be the key to unlocking a healthier me. While watching the sculls slice the water against the setting sun, I was inspired to learn how to sit on a twelve-inch banana peel with two oars and repeat the same feat. My friend Sam introduced me to Darvin, a local fitness guy. Between the two they worked out a health regime that included rowing on the water and on the indoor rowers. Within eight weeks twelve pounds melted away and a leaner me emerged. And a surprise bonus! A tiny lump, as hard as a pea, I found in my right breast.

When I voiced my concerns about what I had felt in my breast, my doctor reminded me that I'd just had a clear mammogram a few months earlier. Fortune placed me next to my mother-in-law, who was also a Ph.D. nurse, at a family dinner two weeks later. I confided in her about my lumpy friend and what the doctor had said. Both her message and her voice are as clear today as they were then.

May 23, 8:05 p.m.: "Henda, no lump is nothing. Have it checked again!"

Per her advice, I called my doctor soon afterward and begged her to please check the lump even though it might be benign. She ordered another mammogram, which was clear again. The screening clinic then wanted to send me home. By now the little voice in my head had become a loud and insistent cry. I refused to leave without checking further. A subsequent sonogram revealed a shadow of enough concern to warrant a needle biopsy. Looking back, I knew I had cancer when I felt the unyielding mass that didn't belong in my breast.

I was diagnosed with breast cancer on June 7 and transferred the next day to the University of Texas Southwestern Medical Center in Dallas. Considered one of the very top hospitals with a National Cancer Institute designation, they performed another mammogram, sonogram, and MRI. In the waiting room I had my first brush with pink, soon to become my favorite color. I was the young one in a room filled with grandmothers. In our bubblegum pink hospital frocks, we resembled an army dressed in really bad uniforms.

The MRI indicated that the cancer had spread to my lymph nodes. The radiologist performing the lymph node biopsy was a kind person who was not about to lie to me. He offered me the one-in-a-million consolation prize: if the MRI was incorrect, and my lymph nodes were *not* involved, my case would be included in the radiology literature of the medical school. No joke. Tell me again how I drew this card?

While I waited for the sonogram, tears ran down my cheeks unchecked. I almost sobbed without restraint when the nurse offered me her own stash of tissues while gently pointing out how hers were softer than the hospital-issued brand. The unreal sequence of events over the past twenty-four hours had dealt me a blow that left me in a zombie trance.

I adore roller coasters. Especially the kind when your throat gets hoarse from your blood-chilling screams as you plunge down the steepest hills into the tightest curves. There are few other places where your own screams are part of such fun. This self-induced punishment always leaves me with less emotional baggage than when I arrived. I wanted to scream that day in the waiting room at the top of my lungs because I was petrified and had no idea of the many twists and turns ahead. More than anything I wanted to get the hell out of the line and not go on the ride. Ever. However, destiny had other plans in store.

June 9, 2:05 P.M.: "Mrs. Salmeron, this is Dr. Rao with UT Southwestern. Is this a good time, and are you sitting down?"

Seriously. Can we please agree that no conversation should start that way? It was the moment that changed everything forever. Dr. Rao, my oncologist surgeon, broke the news to me gently. My tumor was not small, and my cancer was not in an early stage. She wanted me to come back to the hospital right away. We had to consider possibly starting chemo to shrink the four-centimeter tumor before she felt comfortable removing it.

June 9, 3:00 P.M.: Driving back to the hospital. You have to be kidding me! This is not happening! I have two little kids. Would I see them graduate from elementary school? How do I tell them that their mother could be dying? Am I going to die? How did this happen? How did a mammogram miss a tumor the diameter of a golf ball?

I despise cockroaches. Unequivocally, I hate them. They terrify me. The boarding house I lived in with my mother when I was a little girl was roach infested, and they crawled everywhere. Their antennae were always searching for my skin in the dark. Later as a student in boarding school, we had a perpetual roach problem in the bathrooms. You would not dare to walk barefoot in the middle of the night out of terror of stepping on one. I always imagined the "crunch-crunch" if you squashed the little bastards under your shoes. Ugh! I know Pixar tried to make them lovable. To me they are, and always will be, the creepy, scary monster insects from my childhood. My kids can vouch that I run screaming for the nearest chair to climb whenever I see one in my house today.

Apart from cockroaches, darkness had also scared me for decades. Not just any kind of night. The nights when I had to turn the lights out and go to bed by myself. I felt defenseless, certain that some deranged person would attack me while I was asleep. Remember my scissors-clutching nights? Certainly there should be no surprise about this phobia! Additionally, it didn't help that since fourth grade, I'd slept in dormitories surrounded by other warm bodies and in touching distance of another person.

My cancer diagnosis ushered in another awareness of fear—the dread of exhaling my last breath. This was a different league altogether. Suddenly the clichés of living and dying became personally relevant. Like a slo-mo flashback to Nicky's death, my own mortality was staring me down. For one who once dreaded the dark, driving back to the hospital on June 9, 2009, was one of my darkest days.

June 9, 4:05 P.M.: DENSE BREAST TISSUE ... Huh? WTF!

I had never heard those three words strung together. Seriously? Bet you have never heard them either. Try saying "dense breast tissue" a few times fast. It reminds me of a tongue twister like "Sally sells seashells by the seashore." Wish I'd met the person that coined the phrase. Could they have come up instead with "solid," "impenetrable," or "thick" as synonyms to describe breast tissue?

I learned at the hospital that I had very dense breasts and that it was "not the standard of care" to inform women about their breast density. Oh, and by the way, a mammogram can miss a tumor in dense breasts 40% of the time. And, oh yeah, sorry to seem still bewildered, but more than half of women have dense breasts. Those are not small numbers! I'm not making this stuff up. Seriously. Until that moment I had thought "dense" meant "stupid."

It was like a very poorly scripted B-movie, bad jokes and all. I had a baseline mammogram at age thirty-five and faithfully had a mammogram every year beginning at age forty. All my mammograms clearly indicated that I had dense breast tissue, which is why it was inconceivable to me that no one had ever told me.

Are you ready for Breast Tissue 101? There is a quiz at the end of the book so you ought to pay close attention for the next few paragraphs. I still feel like sticking my fingers in my ears and going "la-la-la-la-la," so I know how you are going to feel in about two minutes!

Only a mammogram can reveal the density of a woman's breast tissue. It has nothing to do with your breast size or how your breasts feel. Breast density refers to the proportion of fat and tissue in your breasts. Dense breasts have less fat, and low-density breasts have less tissue and more fat. Still with me? And this fat is not like your tummy or thigh fat that you can lose with a diet. You cannot change your combination of fat and tissue by lifting weights either.

One of the limitations of a mammogram is that dense breast tissue appears as a tight white web on a mammogram, while the tumors that mammography tries to detect are also white. How do you find a tumor on a mammogram when your breasts are dense? Try spotting a snowball in a blizzard. Or find a polar bear in the snow. It is white on white and impossible to see!

Don't get me wrong. Mammograms save lives. Until we can pee on a stick one day for cancer screening, they are the most cost-effective tools in our arsenal on the war against breast cancer. But they are not foolproof. Women must get screened regularly and know their breasts. As advocates of their own health, based on individual risk factors and discussions with their physicians, women should decide what else is prudent.

Don't I sound like a breast density pamphlet or infomercial? The number one reason women don't get screened is fright. Most women are afraid to get the results. Hell. I so totally get it. By the time I left the hospital on the day of my diagnosis, I was a brand-new expert about a subject I'd have rather stayed oblivious about.

June 10, 6:50 A.M.: Screw cancer.

I didn't bother going to bed the night before and had never felt so adrift, isolated, and frightened. I'd received a possible death sentence, and although adversity had been a close friend since I was young, I had no idea what to do. From one hour to the next, it was like an alien invasion of worry that wasn't there before. Terrible "what if" scenarios popped up in little crop circles in my head overnight. Apart from my own demise, I dreaded leaving my two little kids without their mother. Oh, my God. They were only eight and ten. How could this be happening? Hours into this purgatory, some clarity slowly surfaced. I. Am. Not. A. Quitter. And. I. Am. Not. Dead. Yet.

When daylight trickled across my backyard, I silently swore that

I would not rest until I changed the "standard of care." All women deserved an equal opportunity to an early breast cancer diagnosis. By not telling us about our breast density, we lose that chance and could possibly lose our lives! I vowed that was *not* good enough.

Unbeknown to me, in the days, weeks, and months following this night of utter hell, fighting for this cause would become my saving grace. Like a drowning man I grabbed on to it. I redirected and funneled all the anger, frustration, and terror of my diagnosis into this one focal point. This budding crusade against cancer and the establishment created the illusion that I was in control. Those hours from midnight to dawn split me apart and fundamental change from this tender place was launched. Only years later would I fully understand its scope.

June 10, 10:00 A.M.: Mr. Vaught, my name is Henda Salmeron. I had to look you up online, as I didn't know who my local state representative was. And I'm sorry, but I also didn't vote for you. Mr. Vaught, I need you to, no . . . actually . . . I beg you . . . please help me change the standard of care for women with dense breast tissue!

I told Texas Representative Allen Vaught my story and pointed out some of what I'd already learned, namely that almost half of premenopausal women have dense breast tissue. I reminded him we were mothers, sisters, cousins, friends, wives, and often younger women who deserved to know the truth about our breasts. We were not a small minority! He agreed to consider the case. Unclear about the future, I felt that I'd at least tossed my first pebble.

June 17, 9:00 A.M.: "Henda, look what just came over the radiology wires!"

One week after my phone call to my representative, I was prepped and ready to be taken to the OR for my lumpectomy to remove the tumor. My radiologist rushed into my room. She handed me a printout with the news. Connecticut had just passed a bill to inform women about dense breast tissue—the first state in the nation to pass such legislation. I took it as a great omen that my own effort in Texas might not be a futile attempt after all!

After much debate my medical team decided to remove the tumor right away. Although the tumor was large, my surgeon felt confident that she would be able to save my breast. In the first of many decisions I opted out of a double mastectomy. My BRACA gene testing was negative; I didn't carry the breast cancer gene mutation. Not ready to lose my breasts, I chose less invasive surgery. My surgeon also removed my first four sentinel lymph nodes to be examined by the pathologist. If cancer cells were present, all my lymph nodes in my right arm would have to be removed.

Barely a month since my diagnosis, breast cancer was quickly shaping me into a different person. It forced me onto a road where I could see the path but had little knowledge where the way led. I could not have predicted the significant lessons that were waiting.

June 27, 2:30 P.M.: "Sweeties . . . darling bunnies . . . something happened while you were at camp. I got breast cancer."

My cancer diagnosis occurred the week before my kids left for their annual two-week summer camp in the piney woods of East Texas. I was unwilling to send them off to camp with such devastating information. I didn't say a word and had my first surgery while they happily enjoyed the bliss of being carefree kids.

I blurted out my newsflash to the camp directors when we picked them up. By then the tear tracks were well formed down my cheeks.

With a bandaged breast I had no idea how to confess my tumor secrets to my most precious ones. I felt so guilty that I'd withheld the information from them and distressed that they might feel I didn't trust them enough to share. After we exhausted all their camp stories, I finally announced my un-fun update. I had read several books the week before on how to tell your kids you had cancer. But in the moment I just wished that I never had to peel their childhood innocence away. I could tolerate the demands of a breast cancer diagnosis, but it saddened me to be their teacher on this subject of survival.

I held my breath for their response. My ten-year-old son cut to the chase and asked me if I would die. I honestly had to confess that I didn't know. He next questioned what would kill me faster, poison or cancer? Content that I wasn't dropping dead from poison soon, he continued to read his book. My eight-year-old daughter asked if I lost my hair, could I get a wig that looked like her dirty blonde hair? Yeah! No brainer, cherished girl!

The rest of the way home I watched the East Texas countryside pass by, recalling the awe I felt when my firstborn, Mateo, grew in my body. Feeling him move, hearing his steady heartbeat, seeing him on the sonogram screen, and carrying his blurry black-and-white screenshot to show off to everybody. His birth was a small miracle on a very icy December day in 1998 when I held him in my arms. He was just six pounds, three ounces with a head of golden hair—my little love bug.

The wonder repeated itself with my daughter, Dominique, twenty-four months later. Her January birthday was sunny and bright, and she allowed me to have a well-planned delivery day down to a great pedicure beforehand. When I held her moments after her birth, she quenched her thirst from my breasts for more than an hour before she was ready to greet the day. That's my girl—it's not necessary to face anything hungry.

My efforts to teach them independence and resourcefulness started when they were born. It had been hard to watch them stumble so they could learn to get back up. I often had to fight the urge to shelter them, but I knew the importance of learning the art of resilience. I encouraged them to pursue their goals, to be the best they could be, and to seek out what inspired them wholeheartedly. Looking back I suspect it was my calling as their mother from the start. Was I to show them by example what fighting back was all about? Demonstrate how to overcome our biggest challenges? Teach them how to never give up?

Unfortunately I required a second lumpectomy within weeks of my first surgery. It was to ensure that I had what is called "clear margins"—2mm of tissue surrounding the tumor without any cancer cells present. But the enormous homerun I scored? They added me to the radiology case studies because my initial MRI was indeed wrong! Although I had a small cluster of cancer cells in my first lymph node, the next three nodes were clear, allowing me to keep the rest of my lymph nodes. Hell yes! My first of many lucky breaks! And this time my kids were by my side in the hospital.

The following summer when I dropped them off at camp, their hugs proved to be a little tighter around my neck, and my son whispered in my ear, "Mama, please don't let anything happen to you while we are gone!"

One Traveling Bandaged Dense Breast, Late July 2009

DESPERATE TO CLING TO some semblance of normalcy after my diagnosis, (but totally against my doctor's orders), I charged ahead with our plans to spend a two-week summer vacation in Peru. Trekking with the family from the Amazon rainforest to Machu Picchu, Cusco, and the Sacred Valley while recovering from two recent surgeries was dumb. Okay. Plain stupid. Toward the end of our vacation we found ourselves at Lake Titicaca, the highest navigational lake in the world at 15,400 feet. Legend considers it the birthplace of the Inca.

That morning I had my coca leaves read by an old Inca shaman who of course raved about all my good fortune and happiness. He promised that my leaves showed a long life. Uh huh? His smile was too wide for me to tell him about the big "C." Who could tell the future anyway? Maybe he and the leaves were right. Days later from inside an ICU, I would want to ask for a complete refund. Or else some fresh leaves!

On the way to Arequipa, the White City, I had a strange sensation in my chest as if a gorilla were slowly sitting down on me. Each intake of air was a painful exercise of my lungs expanding and collapsing. However, I kept this to myself, thinking that a lower altitude would solve the problem. Besides, Arequipa was our last stop and the birthplace of my father-in-law. I didn't want to ruin the highlight of the trip for my children to see where Grandpa was from.

Our sprawling hotel was located on a river near downtown built in the signature white volcanic stone of the city. But by bedtime I felt lousy, and my breathing difficulty had worsened.

August 1, 9:00 A.M.: "Tu corazón... medio es muerto." Half of your heart is dead.

¡¿Qué?! Come again? I had no doubt that the Peruvian cardiologist standing in front of me was a madman. Only someone insane could utter those words. Me? A heart attack? *Crazy old man!* He rattled on in fast Spanish, way above my basic conversational level, as my mind strained to recall how I had gotten there.

I had woken up that morning at 5:00 A.M. with a rubber tube clasping my lungs in a vise grip. I couldn't breathe, my arms and hands were numb, and I was vomiting. I left my husband behind with our sleeping kids in our hotel room and walked out into the deserted early morning city streets to flag a cab. The Clinica Arequipa was the only private hospital for a tourist like me. In my limited Spanish I instructed the cab driver to head there *"muy rapido!"* I sensed that something was very wrong, but I was optimistic that simply inhaling forced oxygen would restore the struggle of taking a breath. Only later did I realize how dismal my symptoms were.

When I arrived at the hospital I quickly found myself caught in the worst nightmare imaginable. But it was no dream. Instead I was trapped on a very narrow metal cot in the middle of Peru. I had a bunch of needles stuck in my arms and an oxygen mask covered my face. A frantic group of nurses and doctors swarmed around me and I desperately desired for my Spanish to be better.

The cardiologist left after blurting out the status about my half-dead heart. I had an urgent need to escape from there and reached for my cell phone to call my husband... only to find that I had no service! In my haste to catch a cab I had also left the hotel name and number behind. A young intern who spoke English finally came to my aid and offered to find my family. Based on my very vague description of the hotel, he pieced it together and reached Rick. I begged him to hurry to the clinic and could only trust that I would stay alive until he and my kids found me. In the aftermath of a cancer diagnosis, dying in a hallway in Peru was completely unscripted.

My body had been poked and probed the entire summer by my cancer doctors in Dallas. They would surely have picked up on any heart defects? I was careful not to elaborate to anyone about my still-bandaged right breast. There was no reason to heighten the freak-out factor and complicate their focus.

Filled with apprehension, I took the hand of my Peruvian intern and asked, "If I were your sister, what would you suggest I do?" Without hesitation he urged me to be admitted to their ICU and be treated for a heart attack. He reminded me that the EKG clearly showed the event and the cardiac enzyme blood tests confirmed the diagnosis. The longer I stalled, the less chance there was to reverse long-term damage, much less save me from dying. Out of options and stuck in a *Twilight Zone* episode straight from a Halloween special to boost Nielsen ratings, I agreed.

My family's shocked faces mirrored my own when they walked into the makeshift ER a little later. I felt as if all of creation had sucker-punched me hard with some sneaky bitch moves. In the intensive care I was shot full of mystery medicines, swallowed pills without names, and had IV fluids pumped into me. My basic Spanish served no purpose, and I fully surrendered to my caregivers. Their mission was to make sure I didn't die on their watch.

Suddenly breast cancer didn't seem like such a bad deal. At least I could say my goodbyes in an organized way compared to my heart stopping with its very next beat. A vice of sheer panic over my own death clenched me very tightly. I had never been this scared. Ever. I felt lost to my core. The ICU nurse dutifully sat next to my bed while monitoring the machines I was hooked up to. Oh, said machines and ICU were straight from a 1950s movie set! Let's just say that the ICU lacked the glamour and gloss of modern technology. Her English was absent, and I didn't have the energy to try to practice my Spanish. My family stopped by a couple of times a day. But for the most part I was left to drown inside my own mind. I was catapulted back to the hell of June 10 when I didn't think my night could be darker. Only this time I felt myself slipping off the slope out of reach of any shreds I could grab.

Through the small window in my hospital room I could see the El Misti volcano. El Misti is the middle volcano of the three circling Arequipa—the only one still active and holding its place on the Ring of Fire outlining the Pacific tectonic plate. At 19,100 feet its impressive, symmetrical snowcapped peak flirted with me. Out of options about how else to save myself, I made a deal with a volcano, vowing that I would one day stand on its summit. If I survived this ordeal at all.

After three days I was finally considered stable enough for the old cardiologist in charge to clear me to travel to Lima to see a second cardiologist—one who could speak English and was a fellow of the American College of Cardiology. Finally we were cooking with gas! Hallelujah! He alerted the airline, and I flew to Lima in a wheelchair carrying travel permission papers although I had no idea what they said. "Okay, whatever—just get me to Dallas!" I prayed. The Lima doc then blessed my transfer home if Rick would give me anticoagulant shots in my stomach and I would take about ten tablets every four hours. Okay, whatever!

I finally arrived in Dallas two days later—still in a wheelchair and shaking like a ragdoll. We went straight to UT Southwestern. In addition to the breast cancer department, I became fast friends with the cardiology unit. After a string of tests including a heart catheterization, my cardiologist changed the Peruvian doomsday diagnosis to pericarditis—an inflammation of my heart lining. In other words I had just been caught in the perfect storm of wrong place at the wrong time. "Your heart is healthy and strong," he assured me. Alrighty, then! Let the believing begin!

Before my own *Grey's Anatomy* drama-filled episode, our Peruvian excursion had taken us into the dense Amazon rainforest to one of its tributaries. There I bought a simple, hand-carved bracelet for two dollars from another old Inca man while visiting his primitive hut and learning about their customs. It was made from coconut shell and had a woven pattern in the center that reminded me of a spider web. The man used very thin strips of cornhusks to create the pattern, which have slowly unraveled over time. I seldom wear it because it has become very delicate. However, whenever it graces my wrist, it reminds me how fragile our lives are.

Aside from the myocardial infarction (that sounds so much better than a heart attack!), Peru silently initiated me into a love affair with seven great wonders of the world. Our tie would span the next seven years on my own path of discovery and healing. After the

Amazon, the Sacred Valley was our next stop. Sunrise over Machu Picchu debuted the first wonder. Steeped in sanctity and surrounded by mountains bigger than any manmade phenomenon, I reveled in how the sun slowly bathed the age-old ruins in light. And how the mountains leisurely shed their deep purple nightgown for a bright day coat. According to Inca moral code, *Ama suwa, ama llulla, ama quella,* one should not steal, tell any lies, or be lazy. In this sacred place in the Andes, my spirit awakened to strive to live by my own newfound moral code: authentic, vulnerable, and worthy.

But first I had to find the strength in the coming weeks to scale two very large mountains: cardiac rehab and breast radiation. Surprisingly, the universe was also about to upgrade the script from just a B-movie without consulting me first. I was the leading unpaid female in this drama after all!

*The tragedy of life is not that it ends so soon,
but that we wait so long to begin it.*

—W. M. LEWIS

IN MEMORY OF MY FRIEND, LANDON,
WHO FULLY EMBRACED HIS

My Not-So-Finest Hour Eating Darn Fine BBQ!

I HAVE A LARGE hourglass filled with fine white sand. It sits in my living room on a table that was hand carved from a cypress tree near Caddo Lake in East Texas. Every time I pass by it I flip the glass over and allow the sand to trickle through the thin center separating the two delicate bubbles. Occasionally the sand gets stuck, and I must shake the glass for it to drop. I enjoy watching its passage and find satisfaction that I can invert it repeatedly, unlike the ability to reverse events from my past.

My warped sense of humor called for creating a T-shirt to commemorate my 2009 incidents thus far. I thought of "Survived. Despite the market crash." Or how about "Breast Cancer? Heart Attack? Got it!" Or maybe "Held together by spit and duct tape."

My breast cancer radiation treatments had to be delayed while I focused on restoring my heart's full function. Initially I was slated for a twelve-week program at a cardiac rehabilitation complex in Dallas. Reminiscent of the waiting room after my cancer diagnosis, I was the odd one yet again. My companions were grey-haired aging men recovering from stents and bypasses. Together we wore our heart monitors and worked out under the watchful eyes of the nurses and cardiologist on duty. All of us were absolutely committed to the same end goal: a healthy heart.

Fear was my confidante and clung to me. My days evolved into a sick mind game of "which was worse?" Rogue cancer cells growing post-surgery or half a heart? I often caught my fingers on my carotid artery. Instead of counting the beats I would chant with each one "I'm alive, I'm alive, I'm alive." I knew firsthand that when the beat stopped my life would end. It was a reality that I could not swap for the innocence of the clichés about existing in the moment. I had always understood they were true, but I didn't really know how true until we became blood brothers and they crawled into the very fiber of my being.

After four weeks my cardiologist pronounced my heart well and my rehab finished. Easy for him to say! Being OCD came with benefits. I bought a hospital-grade blood pressure machine and monitored my heart at least seven times a day. Imagine a spreadsheet with many rows and columns filled with daily blood pressure data for weeks and months. Now imagine my cardiologist on the receiving end of such information regularly. You really should add him to your holiday mailing list. He is a great man!

Breast radiation followed immediately after my rehab. I was beat up and fed up with all things medicine, and the thought of what was ahead loomed like endless steamy summer days in hell. To start, the target area had to be carefully mapped. The radiation oncologist marked up my right breast and chest with dots and dashes using a black marker to align with the radiation machine's beams. They covered the marks with clear stickers and instructed me to make sure that the stickers stayed put and dry for the duration of treatment. Alternatively, I could opt for permanent tattoos across my skin. Eeewww, where do I check the "No Thank You" box? There was *no* need to turn this into forever anything! Seriously, I would rather have tattooed "I love Rufus" on my bicep than to get my chest radiation marks inked!

They then created a custom mold of my upper body to help me stay in the same position. This aided the accuracy of the beam to pass through my body whilst destroying good and bad cells. Arms raised above my head, I lay on my back as the warm blue fluid in the plastic bag underneath me took the shape of my torso and arms. Afterward they added my name to it, and I was curious whether they might offer it to me as a souvenir at the end.

The traditional radiation protocol called for thirty-six days of treatment, but luckily (and thankfully) I qualified for a shorter, far more concentrated exposure. My last day of treatment was October 2, 2009. By that time my skin was burned from the inside out and peeling badly. It was like having a severe sunburn within every cell inside my body. I was emotionally falling apart and holding on to a very flimsy thread of faith. Time and again, even in my darkest of days, sunlight always looked for a crack to filter through. I just had to keep believing in that single ray of light.

The caution signage on the door to the radiation chamber

reminded me of a scene from a science fiction horror flick. For sixteen days I walked through the door. I lay down on a narrow table underneath the radiation machine, removed my arms from my hospital gown sleeves, and rested into my "Henda" mold. Next the staff aligned the marks and dots with the beast's laser beams. During the next ten minutes the monster machine rotated around my body. It made clicking and whirring sounds like some alien licking its chops before it devoured me. I could never stop my tears flowing down my cheeks in little wet streams. They pooled together in the hollows of my collarbones and formed little eddies that spilled over the edge. How I detested every single one of those sixteen days.

My radiation appointment was every day at 9:00 A.M. sharp. Afterward I walked to one of the oldest barbeque joints in Dallas— the original Sonny Bryan's on Inwood Road across from UT Southwestern. I was usually one of the first customers of the day and ordered a side of coleslaw, two colossal onion rings, and either the pork ribs or slow-smoked brisket. I would slide into one of the snug vintage school desks all lined up in a row and drizzle the warm barbeque sauce over my plate. Although there was no relief from the painful sunburn inside my body, the food brought me comfort and allowed me to briefly rearrange my scattered thoughts. Only years later did I question what my heart was thinking about the daily post-radiation cholesterol pile-up on a plate.

When Lightning Strikes

CROSSING THE STREET FROM my latest nightmare at the hospital allowed me to face my older ones more graciously. My BBQ lunchtime reflections brought me back to the months just prior to my breast cancer diagnosis in June 2009. That spring, before terrible luck and illness altered my fate, depression had swept over me with the unexpected speed and ferocity of a tsunami. I was reluctant to replay those days. But it was as if the scorching heat from the radiation in my chest wanted to ignite my whole being. Its intensity compelled me to re-traverse my old *Way of Sorrows*.

How will I kill myself? It was the most frightening thought that had ever entered my mind. But there it was on a fateful day in mid-February 2009. I was driving down the Dallas North Tollway back to downtown after showing houses in a suburb. I didn't start with asking myself *if* I could commit suicide; instead I contemplated *how*. Knowing myself well, I recognized that my choice of self-destruction would somehow involve my beloved ocean and scuba diving.

My infatuation with scuba diving had begun the week after I arrived in the United States in 1990. Almost 300 dives later, the ocean blue is well acquainted with my issues. It understands how I first float at the surface to let my claustrophobia exhale and breathe. When at ease I can submit to descending into its vastness and discover the gems awaiting me. How magnificent they always are! I've been enveloped in the wings of a stingray, grabbed by a giant octopus's suction cups, and entertained by wild dolphin frolicking.

Humpback whales serenaded me with their complex and haunting songs, indisputably one of the most profound compositions of sound I ever listened to. Cave diving got checked off the list. Once, and only once, did I sink into a cave with hundreds of feet of solid rock above my head. Despite being a self-proclaimed "badass," my bravado evaporated fast when I squeezed myself and my scuba tank through the narrow passages of several underwater tunnels.

Unlike the sinister realm of cave diving, my most favored dive site is a cliff dive, also known as a wall dive. Not only do these locations teem with colorful reef fish, but you can also find large pelagic fish like sharks, rays, jacks, and groupers. My favorite underwater symphony is the melody of my own bubbles mixed with the infinite chatter of fish feeding on the reef. Covered in abundant coral growing vertically on the steep overhangs, the wall can suddenly plunge into the ocean's depth.

While suspended against a wall without any seabed as a barrier, paying attention to one's depth is paramount. Currents can easily sweep you into eternity, particularly if the intent is to never return to the surface anyway. This was my poison of choice. Being a seasoned diver I realized at some point I would become delirious from the nitrogen floating in my blood. In dive slang, the effects of nitrogen narcosis are like one martini for every thirty-three feet of descent. Having dived already to 142 feet in the Blue Hole in Belize on a past dive trip, and following the hypothetical "Martini Law," I figured I would require about five stiff drinks or 165 feet to reach oblivion. My impairment would increase as my depth escalated, and I would slowly lose my judgment to ascend to a shallower depth. The nitrogen narcosis would relieve all anxiety, and instead I would face complete serenity. The selection of my final wall dive would be based on its brilliance. Both in the abundance of marine creatures big and small, as well as its dramatic drops and cobalt blue waters filtering the sun rays to wash the coral reefs into a blooming summer garden.

I was horrified by my thoughts. Contemplating the madness of ending it all was the most foreign place I had ever ventured inside my own mind. I had already lived several lifetimes of overcoming obstacles—quitting on myself should have been unimaginable. How did I get to this desperately lonely place? But more important, how the hell would I get out? Truthfully, I was clueless how to ask for help in one of my blackest hours. I pulled off the highway into a fast food parking lot and sobbed uncontrollably. Despite having a lot of friends, who could I call with this dilemma? It was as if my guardian angels comprehended that it was time for them to intrude fast with a godly intervention.

I dialed Sam. We had not talked in a while, and he seldom answered calls. Miraculously, he picked up on the second ring. I must have sounded worse than I felt as he invited me to come and meet him at White Rock Lake. We sat for a while outside talking on the steps of the old Filter building next to the rowing boathouse. I shared with him the depth of my unhappiness in my marriage, the piercing pain of being caught up in a place I felt like an alien, and the agony of being the most unauthentic person I knew. I finally had the courage to confess that my ongoing project of reinventing "Henda" had gone horribly wrong.

His kindness and wisdom were raindrops falling on my thirsty presence. When I left there I felt I was tossed a life preserver. I had a plan that didn't include a wall dive to eternity. Oh, how thin is that edge between sanity and stir crazy! How narrow that ledge we tread daily. How dark our demons when they are hidden and therefore in charge.

Sam's plan was simple: get me fit. At the time, I felt like (and looked like) a beached baby humpback whale. I weighed almost twenty-five pounds more than my ideal weight today. Being short and small boned does not allow me to hide any pounds in my pockets. I had no muscle definition, and my thighs and upper arms had the familiar jiggle of dimpled cellulite. I can use many excuses as to why and how I'd allowed myself to arrive at the gates of self-loathing. But ultimately it's quite simple. When you avoid your own eyes long enough in the mirror while brushing your teeth daily, you should anticipate self-destruction in some form. My time bomb triggered in 1990 when I boarded the plane to the US and pretended that I was an orphan. Nicky's death in 2006 lit the fuse that led to my winter's depression and the 2009 explosion.

When I'd contemplated how to end it all in February 2009, I had no idea that only a few months later all my guardian angels would quit their jobs. Seriously, how could they let me have breast cancer and a heart attack back to back? After all we had been through together growing up? I'm still mad at them. I needed a serious course correction, but between them, God, the universe, and all the other divine bodies, did they not check in with each other? Or maybe they did. Whatever the case, the strategy worked. Grandly. I'm quite confident they are all smiling fondly down on me these days!

In a cosmic sense of good timing, I hit rock bottom *before* my two-for-one special. My brush with death jumpstarted my ascent. In diving terms I had essentially reached an "out of air emergency" in

February. When you are in deep water and out of air, diver protocol requires that you drop your weights, spread your arms and legs to slow your ascent, and continuously exhale, making an *ahhhh* sound until you reach the surface. Getting to the top, however, is the first of your problems. Your lungs could explode; you can burst all sorts of vessels in your brain. But at least you might make it out alive!

The Stink of Fear

ON MY LAST DAY of radiation I celebrated the finale of torture with a portion of ribs and brisket and a full order of Sonny Bryan's famous onion rings. I was an affirmed mess and very unsure of where to navigate next. I felt betrayed by my very being. The burden to somehow hold it together for my kids and husband was almost unbearable.

In the following weeks it took all my self-control not to just start screaming when friendly grocery checkout clerks asked, "How're you doing today?" My enthusiasm for my real estate career also faded fast. Who cared about selling houses when your heart was about to stop? I felt like a preprogrammed robot each morning: shower, dress, feed the kids, do the laundry, show houses, sell houses, shop for groceries, smile, smile, and smile. (Yelling, shouting, and screaming were not algorithms allowed in the code.)

The intensity of my despair drove me to see a therapist. Referred by a friend, she specialized in post-traumatic stress. I learned what F.E.A.R. stands for—False Evidence Appearing Real. Having never suffered from anxiety I became an expert in another subject quickly.

It was paralyzing. I obsessed about my heart beating and panicked at the very thought of it not beating. My cardiologist let me carry a portable ECG for a month. Every time I felt like I was having a heart attack, the compact electrocardiogram would transmit my heart's reading to a 24-hour monitoring center. Countless times during the day you could find me pulled off on the side of the road with the little device feverishly pressed against my left breast.

The radiation sunburn took a while to heal. My disfigured right breast was a constant reminder that my road to cancer remission was in its infancy. As I imagined cancer cells multiplying throughout my body, I was once again immobilized with the terror of believing that I would be a casualty of the disease. The depth of my anxiety left me powerless. I dreaded waking each day. And my nightly angst when going to bed drove me into the arms of sleeping pills. I felt like such a loser. A quitter. A failure. Half dead, I thought I might as well drop dead.

The therapist encouraged me to treat my terror like a toddler. I could not ignore it. Instead I should give it the attention it was seeking. It was a great analogy because I clearly remembered when my two children had their two-year-old moments of lying flat on their tummies in the grocery aisle while screaming blue murder. Meanwhile I pretended that I lived on one of the shelves and had no idea whose kids they were. *Where was their mom? I mean, really, could she not control her kids?*

How do you pull your ass out of these kinds of thorny thickets? I wasn't sure. Ms. Therapist wanted me to "validate my emotions" and stop thinking that they didn't fit my persona. (Easy for her to say!) She kept telling me that my distress was a "wave I should ride to shore." (Pity I only learned to surf years later!) Ugh, and then we had Step Three. Totally out of reach. Like a balloon that slipped your grasp on its way to the stratosphere. "Be kind to Henda" and "don't chastise yourself for being weak." (But I was brilliant at beating up on myself!) Vulnerability was a foreign place I had seldom visited. Nope. Grit and defenseless were incompatible words never used together in my sentences. How could those guardian angels set me up like this?!

I was three years old again and scared every day. Not just of the dark and cockroaches. I was terrified of dying. I came face to face with the young me—the one who had thought she wouldn't survive either. In a surprising convergence of then and now, I faced the irony of dealing in my own life's currency. The little warrior meeting the old one. My singular quest to just keep breathing made the old crusades against my mother and finding my father appear so infinitely small. My psyche was back in front of the Leadwood tree again seeking guidance—only this time stripped several more layers bare. Without faith or strength I was inexperienced in how to move forward.

The Accidental Making of a Lobbyist

WHILE I WAS LOST in the woods, my state representative, Allen Vaught, was slowly gathering support for the breast density bill that I had begged him to help me author. I certainly was not in any condition to focus on learning political prowess. It was up to him to solidify the right army of supporters. The state of Texas has a legislative session every two years, from approximately January to June. Since the 2009 session was over by that point, we had about a year to prepare to file a bill with the Texas legislature in Austin in January 2011.

In the late fall of 2009 I decided that another excursion to South Africa would brighten my drab and gloomy outlook. Maybe my South African friends could help me practice my latest endeavor of being nice to myself. It was difficult to think my mood could sink any lower, and the thought of spending time in the African bush was very comforting.

The week before my departure I played a card game called Texas Hold 'Em in a charity poker tournament for a local cause. If you are a good card player you don't want me at your table. My decisions are irrational. I fold when I should hold, bluff when I should fold, and generally go all-in when my fate depends on the "river." (The river is the dealer's last card.) I live and die on the river, darling! It either gets me a seat at the final table or a very early night.

On this night fate intervened once again and caused my elimination early on. I found myself next to another doomed player, watching the final ten players duke it out for the big screen TV as first prize. How surprising when I learned he was a seasoned senior lobbyist for a very large national organization. Really? What a coincidence.

I quickly filled him in on the breast density bill and my aspirations to change the standard of care. He tried hard not to burst my bubble, but he was also honest about the political process in Austin. Although my efforts were admirable, he cautioned me not to get my hopes up. In a very kind way, Douglas basically told me that hell would freeze before a highly divided Texas senate and house would pass a breast cancer bill during the first session it was filed. Really? Douglas didn't yet understand that "It's not possible" are words that I thrive on. Additionally, with my insane fright of death, I simply didn't have time to go back for a second or third session. Time was of the essence!

Seeking as much free advice as possible, I speculated aloud how does one pass a bill. Hypothetically speaking of course, but how *does* one pass a bill in one session having had no experience and no money to pay a contract lobbyist? Simple, he said. Buy the book *The Midwest Academy,* study it from cover to cover, and implement each step while lobbying every noteworthy player in Austin. By that he meant the state representatives and their staff, the state senators and all their staff, all the lobbyists for all the major medical groups like the American Cancer Society, the Texas Hospital Association, and the Texas Radiology Society, and every other prominent player that would care about a healthcare bill, which is *everybody*. Learn all their names, he continued, the issues they care about, and try to find a connection so they will give you two minutes for your readymade elevator speech.

Okey dokey! Let's start by begging for Douglas's business card. Intrigued, I also asked what this remarkable book was about. He explained that it teaches the methods and skills to enable ordinary people to actively participate in the democratic process and effectively organize for social justice and change. The day before my flight to Johannesburg, we located the book at a Dallas public library and my husband kindly picked it up. Holy crap! It was enormous! I ended up reading the book cover to cover twice during my two sixteen-hour flights to and from Johannesburg. I reread it during the days while on safari in the bush. In fact it was the only thing that I read during my entire trip. I felt confident afterward that I could pass a multiple-choice exam with extended essays, if quizzed.

Armed with part one of my free advice, I felt comfortable that with Allen Vaught's guidance I could politic my way through Austin. I had a pair of cowboy boots, a blingy belt buckle, and jeans and had also gained a decent ability to dance the Texas two-step and the more progressive triple-step . . . with variations and twirling, might I say. (Really. I'm not lying.) I naively felt that my untrained, unelected, and clueless status would work in my favor. Of course I was marked to fail before I ever started. Just like when I was young. But the underdog and I were old friends at this point. Underestimating me has always worked in my favor and has been my coat rack and umbrella stand in my foyer for half a lifetime.

Meanwhile, radiation had turned my tissues, muscles, and skin into scrambled eggs and ended my rowing. I missed how the rhythm of my oars would carve at the water like a sculptor patiently revealing his creation from stone. While rowing I often found comfort in buckets of sunlight gold across White Rock Lake in the early mornings or occasionally at night. In addition to gold, sometimes I was treated to blood-red stains on the water. Both enveloped me in brief moments of perfect peace. How I longed for those times.

Before my eyes, the last of my rowing muscles vanished as 2009 was ending. Although still slender, I didn't do much exercise past June (understandably, I might add). By December I was worried that my fat clothes I'd stuck in the attic might make a comeback. Luckily my anxiety disorder didn't drive me to food! I was so ready to see the last of this year. For Halloween I dressed as a warrior princess. I guess only I saw the humor in my useless plastic sword—a symbol of how beaten and disarmed I felt on the inside. I could totally visualize me being on my knees, sword against my chest. Okay, high drama, but bear with me... the year was almost done. Had I suspected then what was in store for me, I would have fallen on that imaginary sword!

ACT 3
AFTER CANCER

*To dream anything that you want to dream.
That's the beauty of the human mind.
To do anything that you want to do.
That is the strength of the human will.
To trust yourself to test your limits.
That is the courage to succeed.*

—BERNARD EDMONDS

Arising from the Ashes

THE PAGES OF MY 2009 calendar looked dismal: semi-suicidal and fat in February, Stage 2 breast cancer diagnosis in June, two breast surgeries in July, a heart attack in August in Peru, cardiac rehab and breast radiation in September, severe post-traumatic stress in October and November, complete nutcase by December.

In 2008, just before the start of *Doom: The Ride*, I had rendezvoused with Simone to cheer her on at the finish line of an extreme ultra-endurance race in the Atacama Desert in Chile. Even though I was unfit, unhealthy, and overweight, Simone tried to talk me into participating with her on her next race—an ultra-endurance race that would span seven days and 150 miles self-supported in the Kimberly Outback in Australia a few months later. Whew.

Luckily, despite all the wine we drank, I was smart enough to say no. I imagined the news headlines would have read "Semi-Baked and Half-Dead Humanoid Found by Aboriginals."

Although premature, this small seed of outrageous craziness planted during that very liquid lunch with Simone stayed with me. By the end of December 2009 it became my personal AED (automated external defibrillator) when I searched for a way to shock myself back to living. Out of ideas and with therapy not entirely fixing the mess, this small idea of a big-ass, badass, and crazy-ass "Thing" grew. I needed the "Thing" to be way bigger than my current monsters. The "Thing" also had to be somewhere spectacular and attainable within reasonable limits. I'm so proud looking back that I thought I had any sense and boundaries left in defining the "Thing."

Just before New Year's Eve I stumbled upon the Himalayan 100-mile, five-day stage race scheduled for ten months in the future in India. Imagining the majestic greatness of Mt. Everest was just the kind of "Thing" I desired. Part of me wanted to just click the button on the sign-up page on the website without thinking about it. Man, oh man, contemplating running 100 miles at 13,000 feet in just five days made my feet felt like frozen little stumps from the warm comfort of my kitchen. Clear evidence that I had some sanity left. Then several ironic circumstances unfolded like the opening credits of another movie we should name *Please, Just Go, Girl*.

Although fairly fluent in French when I arrived in the United States, time had rusted my eloquence. In an earlier attempt to burst free of the anxiety-ridden horror I was caught in, I had signed up for French classes near my home for the 2010 New Year. My first class started on the iciest and coldest night in early January. Only the professor and I showed up. With no other students present, my French teacher had much fun clearing some of the cobwebs from my vocabulary. Originally from India, he had grown up in Paris and moved to Dallas a few years previously. His son happened to be in the Himalayas that same night near the small town where the race would begin. Coincidence, huh? Exactly my thoughts.

I turned to my reliable friend Google to delve into the online treasure chest of information about the race. Boy, oh boy, what do you know! I found a previous runner who had competed in the race four times. He lived less than thirty minutes from my Dallas home and after a quick email, we had a two-hour conference call. Who was directing this movie again?

But I was still chicken. The cosmos finally screamed aloud and shoved me into a free-fall when I accidentally came across a documentary at my local video store. I rented *Touch the Top of the World,* the story about Erik Weihenmayer, who was the first blind man to reach the summit of Mt. Everest. Did I tell you all these events occurred in a single week just before the early bird registration deadline?

Out of arguments and excuses, I wired my $2,000 entrance fee and bought an airplane ticket to Delhi using frequent flyer miles the next day. Compared to a marathon or Ironman triathlon, the entry fees for these multiday ultra-endurance stage races are ridiculously expensive. On average you would pay $300-$500 per day for the privilege to carry your own belongings and food, sleep in a communal tent, skip bathing for a week and nurse bleeding feet and aching muscles. While running 140–170 miles over five to seven days through some hot-as-beans desert or jungle. That is before you add in airfare and other travel expenses. As the saying goes, like bacon and eggs you better be the pig and fully committed, as the chicken is just involved and irrelevant.

My expectations were high that India, the Himalayas, and I were destined to dance together at the Henda Revival party. Other than sheer coincidence, I often ponder what drove me to this race. Desperate people do desperate things. When I signed up I was hopeless. After years of being my own gatekeeper, I had no real plan for how to save myself. Dreadfully lost, I hovered on the edge of lunacy and depended on the complete irrationality of this race to offset the other. I felt like I was straddling my fault lines with my sanity about to implode. Could this race deliver me from the shadows? Only twice before had I faced such a compelling sense of utter self-saving, once when I went to boarding school and once when I came to America. We can argue that this time was far more essential.

Let's read the fine print together, shall we? I had never run any marathon. Nope. Nada. Not even a 5K race. The last time I ran in an official capacity was the 4x100m relay in high school. Although I had lost twelve pounds with my initial efforts earlier in 2009, I was still considerably unfit and a little fat for any race, not considering 100 miles in India.

At the time I took tennis lessons from my on-again-off-again trainer, Darvin. Our initial coaching, of course, got interrupted by "crappy chest events." We were playing tennis with sponge balls to help me rebuild my muscles on my right side post radiation. Sitting cross-legged on the tennis court on a cold January morning, I disclosed the "Thing." Kudos to him for hiding his shock and even more praise for tentatively agreeing to help me prepare! We came up with a strategy that was simple and sound: make me strong enough to walk the whole race and get to the finish dead last, as there were no cutoff times for each of the five stages.

Patience, Grasshopper! (Master Po, Kung Fu)

OKAY. WHERE DO WE start to train me for a 100-mile race? Sponge tennis balls were not going to get my ass up and down those mountains. Shortly after my impulse buy of a couple thousand bucks, the truth hit home that Dallas is 430 feet above sea level. We've already established that my math proficiency is compromised, but even I could do the subtraction that 12,570 feet of serious trouble loomed ahead. Years ago, while in high school, I attended a weeklong survival camp and learned how to leopard crawl through the bush. Having it as my race backup plan, in case my running/walking failed, made me feel slightly less panicked.

Darvin instructed me to buy a pair of trekking poles. Feeling kind of silly, I walked with them at White Rock Lake. One mile was so far! Initially that was all I could handle. My first champagne-worthy victory encompassed me walking around the entire White Rock Lake. The near ten-mile hike took me only 2.5 hours to complete! Hell, I packed an overnight bag "just in case"—I'm kidding! When I crossed the bridge separating the east from the west bank in late January 2010, I felt the birthing pains of a possible athlete. Well. I'm sort of a half-full glass kind of a chick.

Many round-trips later, the landmarks around the lake I had driven by so often had become familiar sites at eye level. By late spring my jiggle had also been replaced with the virgin blossoming of muscle definition. Seriously, not fudging. I didn't quite carry six-pack abs yet, but I was certainly working on two small bottles of something. A few side benefits emerged. Sort of the law of unintended consequences. I learned to be patiently alone with my thoughts. All of them. After about three months and lots of miles together, we became somewhat friends. Not close friends. More like neighbors dropping off cookies or a pie during the holidays. I was still mad at them for disintegrating to where I had to go run 100 miles in India to restore our togetherness. But we were making progress. It helped that I had all the trees beside my route around the lake to talk to. They became close friends and the mute spectators of my growing strength and endurance.

I don't meditate. Trust me, I tried. I did Bikram yoga for a few months and couldn't handle the smell of fifty people's sweat around me. I attempted regular yoga as well but just didn't find the yogi supposedly residing inside me. I struggled a few times to sit cross-legged while staring into a flower and a flame during 2009. I couldn't contain my thoughts. Like obnoxious puppies, they ran everywhere. But chained to three hours of walking and talking to myself? I found my meditation. That place where I can connect and converse with my insides. Mano y mano. My sacred mantra of keep moving forward just one more mile was born at White Rock Lake.

Regarding that elevation business. The steepest Dallas incline resembling a smallish hill was the spillway near the wall of the dam at White Rock Lake. Even with a weighted pack to strengthen my muscles, my ultra-endurance athlete visions were on very thin ice from the start. Darvin instructed me how to traverse the hill. A few times a week I trekked up and down its little slope pretending I was on a real one. Against its unevenness I could feel the pebbles, rocks, and soil give under my weight just enough to make me aware I was walking on earth and not pavement. My trekking poles acted like my second pair of feet, and I felt as if I moved on four legs as I completed my first 100 repetitions.

While I traversed the hill I noticed the many tiny grasshoppers jumping everywhere around me. Considering a regular-sized grasshopper's jump can exceed three feet, equally speaking, I would have to execute a standing long jump of about 120 feet! Such infinite might for their size! Although we're told to smell the flowers on our way, we might be better off finding company among and listening to the grasshoppers instead. No worries, by now I was also comfortably talking to a few egrets, blue herons, and a large flock of geese and ducks. By the time I left for India I could have opened my own Doctor Doolittle office.

The other casualty of trying to become an endurance athlete was my closet. As if overnight, my high heels competed with at least five pairs of running shoes. My oversized skirts, dresses, and pants formed their own showroom at Goodwill as I had to donate almost every bit of clothing I owned. The grocery store missed me in the center aisles when I abandoned their collection of processed, canned, boxed, and packaged goods. Instead I hovered on the outskirts of the store and loaded my cart with ingredients that swam, grazed, or grew in good, healthy soil and water.

My resting low-fifties morning heart rate called for my newfound health to rejoice from the inside. The only reminders to the previous summer from hell were the still red-ridged scar over my right breast and the lingering pain in my chest area from the radiation treatments.

Sunday morning, April 11, 2010. An epic date. My first race, a half-marathon in Dallas called The Big D and the birth of another addiction. The energy at the start line pulsated through me and electrified every molecule I owned. It unleashed a powerful adrenaline high that I would come to feed again and again in the years to come. I also confirmed that I belonged to a village called Just in Case. My smallish race pack carried enough supplies to last more than 100 miles instead of thirteen miles on streets near my house. Just in case . . . I carried three bandage rolls, some moleskin, scissors, a handful of bandages in different sizes, two pairs of socks, an extra pair of running shoes, a long-sleeved T-shirt, a few energy bars, some toilet paper (got to be prepared!), sports gels, and water. I got that the race organizers handed out plenty of water and some energy food and bananas at water checkpoints. With thousands of runners, I was worried that they would be out by the time I arrived somewhere near dead last. Except for an umbrella that wouldn't fit in my bulging pack, I felt prepared.

Uuugghhhh! As the total rookie, idiot, clueless running klutz I was, a few days before the race, I ran into pain during a run around the lake. With my calf cramping badly, and not having the smarts, I kept running for another few miles. It finally dawned on me that just maybe, something a little more serious than a cramp caused my discomfort. After a calf sonogram, I learned about tears. Bloody hell! I refused to think a calf tear would stand between my first race and my first potential finisher medal. I had to prove to myself I could complete a half-marathon. With or without pain. At the last minute I slipped two hydrocodone pills left over from my breast surgery into my pack.

Initially I kept a pace of four miles an hour, and before I knew it I passed the five-mile marker. All systems were still green. The inclines reminded me that my calf was not 100%, and I dutifully slowed down. Near mile marker ten, a beacon crossed my way. Tired and keeping my eyes peeled on asphalt, I spotted pale purple flowers scattered around my feet. It was a jacaranda tree covered in spring flowers! In Dallas! I crossed the finish line with a makeshift jacaranda garland twined around my running belt and the incredible joy of a long-lost lavender memory. My infatuation with race bling emerged then too when my first race medal was placed around my neck.

Wilderness Musings

LET'S NOT FORGET THE blood pressure machine that I had bought following my MI (that attack thing)! It still lives happily next to my bed. Instead of multiple daily checks, these days I tamely test my blood pressure only a few times a month. Weird, agreed. Okay. I'll let you in on a secret that I really should save for later in the story. I'm still a little terrified of dropping dead. It has become part of my quirk list. Since 2009 I've tried to become a "here and now" person. My friend Darvin puts it best. It's like we die each night, and rise each morning anew with the sun. Although I have long-term care insurance, I don't really believe that I'll get old. My kids are on board that I never want to sit in a diaper, strapped to a chair while being spoon-fed. Ever.

In addition to the blood pressure machine, I have a few other members of a motley bedside crew on my nightstand. My angel's name is "Courage." Although petite, she has wire wings, a single raised arm, and a wooden body. She guards me from my own darkness. She was gifted from a friend during my cancer radiation and lost her right arm in a tragic accident while I was house cleaning one day. Looking at her daily, I'm reminded that if I continue to confront my fears, I can prevail. I find great comfort in seeing her remaining arm boldly raised victoriously above her head. While preparing for India, I visualized that I would also raise my arms in victory at the finish line with a heart happily ticking away.

I have three pebbles next to her. I stole them from a local Asian restaurant in Dallas many years ago. Each pebble represents ten summers. Initially I had eight pebbles totaling eighty summers in a fortunate person's life. I tossed out all my used-up ones, which left me with three pebbles next to my bed. Seeing them daily reminds me how precious each day is and how urgently I want to execute my goals and realize my ambitions today. And get to blow out eighty candles on a cake with an intact mind and body! Maybe one day if I'm lucky.

Let me introduce you also to my bedside frog. He is small and made from a rich golden-brown wood. I found him in an African arts and crafts market in Johannesburg. His creator carved ridges on his back and he came with a small wooden stick. When I roll the stick over his spine, the sound is a perfect "ribbit." Frogs are symbols of prosperity, wealth, and abundance in Asia. But that's not why he lives next to my bed.

One of my simple pleasures is listening to the outdoor frog concert during the balmy summer nights in my backyard. It's a wild, loud, and crazy get-together of some of the showiest amphibian artists in Dallas! They soothe me with their tunes and compel me to *salud* the living, and the utter greatness of such very tiny creatures making some incredibly big noise. I should take my blood pressure readings during their nightly performance. I bet my cardiologist (and I) would worry less. I enjoy just holding him in my hands and slowly playing ribbit tunes on his back, making me an honorary member of my backyard summer band. I also wouldn't pass on any luck he happened to impart either.

As we discussed, Dallas is no place to train for altitude. To compensate I scheduled a couple of Colorado stays in the summer of 2010. Real, big-ass mountains with nosebleed altitude were my marching orders from Darvin. My friendship with the Rockies had been mostly limited to blankets of snow at that time. I had easily reached their drenched-white peaks, whisked upward by ski lifts while freezing my buns off. My brief pauses from the summits to admire their expanse lasted only enough to contemplate my ski tracks down the steep mountain runs. I carved snake patterns with my skis through soft white powder when I dared to find a line between the trees. The black runs and moguls fondly watched while I gallantly attempted to appear graceful whenever I wiped out grandly. Imagine a yard sale of flying skis, poles, legs, and arms tumbling down a slope! That would be me.

This time my own feet would have to traverse the mountain trails upward to where the wildflowers bloomed in the crisp breeze. It was early summer and the villages still lacked visitors flocking all over. I picked my first route with care and planned to cross the Continental Divide at a maximum elevation of 12,500 feet. The local guide warned me there might still be ice above 10,000 feet and that mud and water from the melting snow could affect my nine-mile hike.

The trail was a mere twelve inches wide and went straight up. Right away I stopped several times to admire aspen forests, pine trees, and mountain streams. My iPod was somewhere in my pack and turned off. Why would I disturb this incredible feast that God had prepared for me with mere music? My Nikon added extra weight to my eight-pound pack, but I had refused to embark on this memorable event without it.

I had my usual array of JIC snacks and emergency gear with me. Just in Case. Although I often endured teasing for carrying a convenience store in my pack, food had become vital to me on extended training days. I looked forward to stopping to munch on a cheese stick or some delicious dried apricots, bananas, cereal bars, cherries, or the ever popular "tuna to go." Sitting under a majestic tree next to a mountain stream to mix tuna with the little packets of mayonnaise and sweet relish was the equivalent of five-star dining!

Onward and upward. Snow soon covered my tracks and the only choice short of turning back was to push through it. I tried to follow the boot prints of earlier trekkers in the day, but the ground melted from the bottom, and with each step I risked sinking to my knees in slush. Without sturdy boots, my shoes, socks, and lower pants legs were soaking wet fast. The mountains thawed with each step. Higher up the snow became thicker and only the faint boot prints of previous days indicated where the route might be hiding.

Once I cleared the thickness of the alpine forest, the most unbelievable view rewarded my progress. Surrounded by white-capped mountain ranges, a frozen lake, and alpine woods, I could only admire God's handiwork in complete awe. Blue skies flirted with storm clouds as the sun barely peeked out its head. Birds and butterflies played chase and I felt as if I could just open my own wings and glide in the mountain breeze. The discomfort of frozen feet and wet clothes was inconsequential. Reluctantly I turned around to descend in my own footprints.

My thoughts were all I had for company against the backdrop of the stunning Colorado panorama. Surrounded in its vastness, I was introduced to the peaceful refuge where my mind learned to be still. I was unprepared for the emotional toll that the trails took on me. Many nights I almost fell asleep in my dinner plate, totally spent. My final Colorado day ended after seven hours, fifteen minutes, and twenty-four miles across the steep expanse. Physically, this final trek confirmed that I had slowly built my endurance over the many months of training, and that high altitude was not an enemy. But the mental drilling contained the greater value. Understanding how to spend eight hours a day unaided in the woods with my own thoughts was a novel place to linger. Unwittingly, it would become part of my daily bread in the Himalayas.

How far I had come from the girl sitting on the tennis courts on a cold January day aspiring to see the sunrise over Mount Everest and running 100 miles over five days. I had never confronted the vast American wilderness as I did during those lengthy summer days. I was isolated for many hours, walking without meeting anybody. Switchback after switchback, hour after hour, treacherous descents followed steep uphill climbs—the trails unyielding, each step a twisted ankle waiting to happen. I learned to just be. It took several more years before "Let Be" became more than just a pipedream. But the comfort of being alone with my twisted side was born that summer in the mountains of "Colorful Colorado." Like lovers who will never forget a special caress, they touched me intimately with their magic. They branded me as mountain worthy and helped me to feel I had a small chance to cross the finish line in the Himalayas.

My goal for the Himalayan 100 was very simple: Finish it. Last or not. Who cares? My playbook was from the African bushmen to just walk, walk, run, walk, run, walk, sleep, eat, walk, run, walk, walk some more. Keep moving my legs and feet until I reached the finish line. (Although the bushmen never had a finish line and just kept walking!)

No impending visit to India would be complete without the recommended vaccination cocktail and I got them all: hepatitis A, typhoid, meningitis, tetanus, polio, diphtheria, pertussis, seasonal flu, swine flu, and malaria tablets for the road. Just before I left for the airport I squeezed my three bedside buddies into my race bag. Scaling the Himalayas with a frog, an angel, and three pebbles seemed very appropriate.

Curbside Bulk Trash Pick-Up

I SNUGGLED COMFORTABLY INTO the soft warmth of my pillows and waited for daybreak to catch up to me. Freshly bought pillows, I might add. I contemplated what I was going to pack for my upcoming adventure to India.

I have alluded how much I hate packing suitcases and thought I would expand a little more about my shortcoming. I'm unable to plan what I want to wear, much less consider what the weather will be at the given time. My vocabulary does not include "light" or "mix-

and-match" and large feelings of inadequacy make me avoid the pain to the very last minute. I then cram, stuff, and fill my suitcase with unnecessary things that I don't have time to sort through. My "Just in Case" genetic wiring also lets me grab the largest suitcase possible and stuff it with everything short of a farm sink.

My one shining luggage achievement? In 2009 I packed my children for their annual summer camp in the back of our SUV while my husband drove. Distracted and distraught by my cancer diagnosis, the week prior had slipped away. The camp was three hours away. On the day I crammed their unpacked trunks and all their belongings into the back of our Suburban. I packed a trunk for each kid while name marking every item—clothes, towels, toiletries, linens, and all else needed for two weeks away from home. Although I was a short-lived phenomenon, my chest still swells with pride at the memory of pulling into the camp parking lot with two well-packed trunks!

As the first sunrays teased my bedroom drapes, I conjured what the emotional baggage I dragged around with me weighed. With any luck India could turn my "medical" bag into something on wheels that was easier to transport. For now, it was immovable. My other bags were not carry-on potentials either. However, by telling people (you) about them, maybe I could shed some of the burden.

About Mother. We haven't talked about her lately and must revisit the drama. Her bag comes with hefty excess weight charges. Can you believe I was still dragging it around at this point? For years I refused to even acknowledge that I owned it. The many hours in my own head while running around White Rock Lake gave me the courage to pick it up, open it, and start to remove the junk from it.

Its explosive force required me to treat it with the respect one reserves for an unclear minefield in Angola. Let me repeat after me: "I'm an accomplished, successful, confident, and well-adjusted woman with the welts from being discarded, neglected, and abused as a child." It is the weight of the shame and guilt from being unwanted, of not being enough, that makes this so heavy. I recognize today that it was neither my faults nor my shortcomings that caused me to be left as a child. My goal is to one day leave this bag empty for bulk trash pick-up on the sidewalk. It should not be lugged anywhere. I secretly fantasize about burning it—pour the gasoline, strike the match, and watch the flames while sipping extremely expensive French champagne.

A few years ago I moved my physical real estate office. While packing up my filing cabinets I came across the infamous letter that Mother wrote to me just before my wedding about who my father was. I had forgotten I'd kept it, and for days it burned a hole in my desk drawer. Should I read it one last time? Toss it out unread? Move it with me to the other office and let its words continue subsisting, albeit securely trapped in a metal drawer?

I read it one last time and afterward shredded each page piece by piece. By tearing the words apart I hoped that I could get rid of some of the pain inside me. Much time had passed since then and I still didn't have a clue how to share the information I'd found within its pages. I told very few people about it, avoided talking about it, and tried never to think about it. In part my trepidation was locked in my belief that it was just another lie. Dad, Daddy, my dad . . . these were words I had never used to express my love for the man that helped to create me. It was such a dark and empty hole on my inside. It reminded me of when I dived my deepest dive in the famed Blue Hole in Belize. It is more than 350 feet to the bottom and we maxed at 142 feet. There was nothing to see. But looking up to its mouth, hammerhead sharks were circling against the sunlight. I felt it was another message from my much-loved ocean. Native Hawaiians consider hammerheads to be gods of the sea and protectors of humans. What the heck did we do before Wikipedia?

Checked bag number two. Its nickname is "trapped." I have been schlepping it around for a while. Since being diagnosed with a potentially fatal disease in 2009, I don't see its retirement any time soon. I suffer from the distress of being stuck in an unfulfilling existence, imprisoned in a world requiring me to conform to rules and regulations I object to. The pedestrian day to day causes me to feel locked in a cage that I cannot escape from. I find the effort to adjust to the tedious everyday particularly taxing. I'm petrified that I will run out of time today before I'm ready to go wherever we go next. Every day becomes a race—a crucial and urgent rush to spend my time well, to do the things that count the most. To squeeze in as much living as I can. I focus on the awe of being alive and the marvel found around me each day. I was once accused of having trouble with the mundane. Yes! Utterly. I refuse to emphasize anything mundane! I do the laundry, shop for groceries, clean my house, make my bed, prepare dinner, run errands, drag my trashcans to the curb every week. By the way, I despise that chore! I always forget that it's trash day and only remember when I hear the city garbage trucks coming down the road. Between opening my gate and rolling them outside in time are angst-filled moments. Trust me. I *can* do mundane. I just choose to focus on the new day, the smell of fresh rain, the fall colors, and the spring flowers and leave mundane in a supporting role.

My last bag is a crazy, overstuffed, rugged, and worn duffle—yet not necessarily one I'll ever get rid of either. You can always squish a duffel into a tight space. Badly packed and full of unnecessary items, mine is filled with my personal chaos—so much that I must sit on it to close the zipper.

The list is lengthy. Let's start with over-commitment. Like having a spare arm, I can visualize 29.5 hours in a day. I walk around with notecards, scraps of paper, and sticky notes filled with to-do lists. Electronic organization failed me years ago. I panic more effectively when I carry a stack of paper citing what is still undone. Mix in a double dose of impatience. I don't consider patience a virtue. I think it's a concept that interferes with multitasking and prevents me from getting rid of said paper.

The duffel is also filled with things like road rage, frustration with bad service, unwillingness to accept a steak that is not medium rare, "no, it's not possible," bad pillows, stinky towels, clutter, potholes causing flat tires, dirty sinks, light switches without dimmers, and automatic computer restarts before I can close the fifty internet search windows I have open—just to name a few. And dust. In the same way that socks disappear in the wash, dust appears from nowhere. I recently looked up "where does dust come from?" and was amazed by the answer. Most of it is dead skin cells, fibers from clothing and other material, pollen, dander, and tiny particles of dirt. Dust comes from objects in the environment, and from the people and animals that live in it. Gross!

Our quirks make us the unique and marvelous beings we are. Like our fingerprints, no two people share the same combination of peculiarities. I own mine proudly. Feel free to change your toilet paper back after I leave your party. You won't hurt my feelings because it may bug you all the way to bedtime!

I desire to have nicely packed bags where everything is organized neatly. I fantasize about just having a carry-on that can be placed under my seat. I want to travel light, free from excess baggage fees. Still unsure about what to pack for India, I knew that my stomach carried a bunch of butterflies. I was excited, nervous, and hopeful. I could only trust that India was ready for an American African looking for her "Thing."

*If we look at the world with a love of life,
The world will reveal its beauty to us.*

—DAISAKU IKEDA

Wondrous Love

MY PREVIOUS LONG-HAUL FLIGHTS to South Africa had always taken me back to the womb or introduced me to life in a sardine can. Tightly squeezed into a coach seat, I could never decide which one as I folded my limbs into several fetal positions while trying to find comfort. To kick off my Indian expedition, I used frequent flyer miles and upgraded to business class instead. I found myself comfortably cocooned inside a Boeing 777 next to a Tibetan monk dressed in a saffron robe, its flamboyant hues belying the wearer's simple lifestyle. We chatted about the Himalayas while dining on tandoori chicken with fenugreek, lemon rice, and kidney beans in a cardamom yogurt sauce. My meal, although delicious, reminded me that I was crossing two oceans and several continents to get from Dallas to Delhi.

I hugged my kids fiercely at the airport and blindly trusted that one day they would understand why I had to leave them for three weeks to very-far-away. Just nine and eleven then, their existence was a simplistic sequence of safety and routine. It was my first extended absence from their day-to-day, but I froze enough crockpot stews for several months! I certainly created a lasting memory of freezer-safe containers containing the uncertain color of beef, pork, or chicken. My sticky notes taped to the lids were the only clues to what was for dinner. (My daughter eloquently describes the frozen separation of protein, fat, and sauce. Shame. Poor baby. Her therapist one day will have to heal those issues!) As I boarded my flight I fervently whispered my prayer to reclaim my spirit so I could be a better version of the current me for them.

Night was in full swing when I cleared customs in Delhi. Exiting the airport, my lungs shuddered at their first intake of densely polluted air. Wow. I never knew exactly what tasting and swallowing dirty felt like. Maybe Delhi should consider hosting the Olympic summer games! Didn't it improve Beijing's air quality? My B&B hotel was tucked away on a small side street and the TripAdvisor reviews were spot on. You were treated like family. Over ice-cold Indian beer and a communal dinner of mutton curry, rice, and naan, I felt immediately at home. We shared stories about cricket, Durban surfing, curry dishes, and the recent Commonwealth Games. Indian culture played a large role growing up in South Africa. Durban, six hours away, was the nearest beach to my hometown of Pretoria and was home to one of the largest Indian communities outside of India. Gandhi had spent many years there as a young man. Without any language barriers since everybody spoke English, my connection to my hosts was quick. I announced my plan to take the public Agra train the next day to the Taj Mahal. It was quite comical to observe the sheer horror on their faces. I'd had no idea what public trains in India held in store for a single female traveler while planning my itinerary. It didn't take much for them to convince me to opt for a driver instead.

Early the next morning my Indian road trip commenced with Espy, my private driver arranged by the B&B owner. I once thought traveling the Pan-American Highway as it winds through the rainforest in Costa Rica was psychotic, but it was nothing compared to the complete insanity I witnessed. Being roadworthy simply suggested you had wheels or legs of some sort that could move. There were buses, trucks, tractors, cows, bicycles, motorcycles, cows, pushcarts, rickshaws, tuk-tuks, scooters, camels, donkeys, horses, and pedestrians (did I mention cows?) all sharing the road and completely ignoring the lanes and direction of traffic. Espy's agility behind the steering wheel earned my heartfelt admiration. The dodging and maneuvering, while honking almost the entire way, was worse than a migraine. Amid the chaos, Espy's cell phone would routinely inform him in a very sexy and sultry voice: "Darling, you have a new message waiting for you."

I counted four people on a tiny motorcycle, fifteen people smashed into a tuk-tuk that should only carry six at most, and saw a mattress being carried on a bicycle between two women. Entire families sat squashed on top of two wheels with the kids desperately hanging on. And about the cows in India. I had never seen calmer cows contentedly and effectively evading traffic. I realized that the dairy advertisements in the US were lying: happy cows don't live in California!

The flamboyant hues and intricate designs of women's saris

were exuberant splashes across the otherwise dreary and grey scene. Combinations of chartreuse and a rich periwinkle reminded me of bouquets of hydrangeas scattered and spilled over the streets. Others in lush red, orange, and yellow fabrics created an Oz-like meadow. Like Dorothy and her companions in the field of poppies, my jet-lagged eyes had to fight staying awake.

Before we reached Agra we stopped at Mathura, revered as the birthplace of one of India's most popular gods, Lord Krishna. Espy's English was not the easiest to follow and I totally misunderstood his "up the hill, then right and left" directions. He had to park some distance away and sent me off to find the temple. Lost, I soon found myself in uncomfortable surroundings. Of course, blending in was difficult. I kept my eyes firmly stuck on the dirt underfoot and wanted to summon Lord Krishna to steer me directly (and quickly) to my destination. It was my first exposure to the relentless onslaught of beggars, vendors, guides, and drivers offering me their services. The Indian humidity swiftly transformed the weight of my backpack to that of a smuggler toting gold bars. My sweat poured like a rainstorm in the desert—fast, furious, and drenching.

After a quick tour of the temple I reunited with Espy and we sped onward to Agra and the Taj Mahal. He dropped me near the entrance and suddenly it was in front of me: the Taj Mahal, one of the Seven New Wonders of the World carved entirely from ivory-white marble and precious stones. Seeing its scale and architectural perfection up close was awe inspiring. No picture could ever do justice to its flawlessness and luster.

As I turned the corner to enter the grounds, my bliss bubble violently exploded. Holy cow! There were thousands of people swarming the entire compound! You had to be kidding me! My struggle with large gatherings is legendary, and in my completely exhausted state I could not contemplate joining the throng. Being short, crowds make me severely claustrophobic. They fold down over me and it's as if I can hear all their hearts beating simultaneously and feel the air thinning with too many breaths taken at once. "But it's the Taj, dummy," half of me was arguing, "MOVE!"

I unwillingly approached the serpentine line that was several layers thick while stretching across the front terrace like multiple switchbacks on a steep mountainside. Only a handful of foreign tourists were present. My visit coincided with a major national vacation and I had never considered that half of India would be present to share in my love fest. Inside the tomb chamber, the pushing and shoving and heat radiating from hundreds of bodies tightly pressed together was almost more than I could bear. I made my escape quickly and stumbled upon a side hallway and recessed arch that was remarkably empty. I rested my cheek and hands against the cool marble and grasped why the Taj was described in my guidebook as a vision, a dream, a poem, and a wonder.

In this private space I could finally hear the romance and adoration softly spoken within. As I traced the filigreed walls, delicately carved from a single marble block, I thought of the love that Shah Jahan (a Mughal emperor) had had for his favorite wife, Mumtaz Mahal. She died in 1631 while giving birth to their fourteenth child and he commissioned the Taj to house her tomb. In all honesty, if I had to bear fourteen kids, I would expect nothing less than a marble monument in return. Among the many inlaid stones, the red carnelian's fire burnt like their story of loss. The lower walls, carved in a relief of flowering plants, highlighted the texture of the polished marble under my fingertips.

Dusk was falling as I exited and the translucent marble was aglow in soft orange. I lingered a while in the gardens under the fragrant trees, tucked away from the masses so I could enjoy unobstructed views of this universal symbol of devotion. I felt my own shortcomings in understanding the depth of such affection between a man and woman and the sorrowful despair of its loss. Recent events had revealed some visible cracks in my own marriage. We had built a good life together, had two spectacular kids, and certainly enjoyed the many conveniences of being married. But I sensed that we lacked the commitment to build a memorial as an expression of our undying love.

Outside the gates of marble splendor, the stark reality of India's poor surrounded me once more. Many were children and even more were crippled, missing limbs and showing terrible signs of illness and malnutrition. Hell was defined in the sadness of their eyes and within their vacant stares of complete hopelessness. They reminded me of packs of stray dogs aimlessly roaming the streets looking for the smallest scraps. I clearly appreciated why I had been advised to get the variety of vaccinations, including polio, before my departure.

As I made my way with Espy to my hotel, Mother Teresa's mission reverberated off the buildings and down the alleys. I could hear her urging to care "for the hungry, the naked, the homeless, the crippled, the blind, the lepers . . . all those people who feel unwanted, unloved, uncared for throughout society, people who have become a burden and are shunned by everyone." I was afforded a very small glimpse into such a world when I was young. But unlike so many less fortunate, my outcome was blessed by a multitude of friends willing to comfort, aid, and catch me.

Despite the destitution, marigold garlands adorned everything from tuk-tuks, temples, and shacks to cows. Like drops of sunlight, their blooms lessened the starkness around me. My hotel presented me with a garland when I checked in, and my bed was decorated in even more golden yellow. Dead tired, I surrendered to the incredible comfort of my pillow. Bypassing dinner, I was asleep before 9:00 P.M. My first full day in India had come to a fitting close.

Indian Rhapsody

ESPY DROVE ME BACK to Delhi the next day and I caught my flight to Mumbai. How sensuously does the word roll on your tongue? *Mumbai, Mumbai* . . . it invoked a wonderful beat in my body. One I wanted to take dancing all night. Having tried many styles of dance including the tango, Spanish flamenco, ballet, jazz, ballroom, and Latin, I knew that Mumbai could only be fun!

Leaving the airport, I was indisputably in the tropics. The humidity in the air immediately folded itself around me like a long-lost lover. In one of my less bright moments, I prepaid for a cab ride to my hotel while inside the airport. In a second of total madness I agreed I had no preference between a car with or without air conditioning. (Henda, sweetie: serious dumb move, darling!) I was whisked into a very small, very old, and without AC little black and yellow rattletrap—let's not insult cars here!

All four windows were down and within minutes I was boiling

hot. Was it too late to hitch another ride in air-con? Palm trees and other tropical foliage dressed up the slums outside the airport and softened the harsh reality of the depressing poverty all around. We snaked along, surrounded by incessant honking, as we squeezed into any traffic gap. Rapidly my eyes burnt like an inferno and my lungs shuddered to take in the densely polluted air and exhaust fumes.

The now familiar Indian sweat-storm dripped down my body, creating large, damp patches on my clothes. I worried how long the transfer to the hotel would take. I was hopeful that it would either be short or that someone would shoot me on the way. We pulled into the Westin Mumbai Garden City about forty-five minutes later. Unsteady, I staggered out of my self-imposed vapor torture. I needed a drink.

The hotel had been recently built, but the realities stemming from the 2008 Mumbai terrorist attacks were evident in the metal detectors I passed through before entering the hotel. It was barely ten o'clock in the morning and I recognized there was a slim to no chance I could check in that early. But what do you know? The Indian gods rewarded me for my unwise airport transport and my room was ready. Judging from the lobby there was nothing shabby about this place and "a lush and splendid oasis" were true words from their website.

My room was on the 28th floor. Behold! Upgraded to the executive level and a suite! YES! No complaints here! Exhaustion can be sly and sneak up quickly. My own fatigue, both mental and physical, had been accruing over time. How I craved a time out and Mumbai offered a brief reprieve from all of it. Pampered and lounging in a robe doing little to nothing vs. keeping the sightseeing deities happy? What do you think! Room service and a nap vs. rushing around the city? My mind was made up when I saw the slogan on the hotel information booklet: Feed the body. Nourish the soul.

My spoiling continued with a sixty-minute body scrub and a ninety-minute massage at the fabulous spa downstairs. The body scrub of cane sugar, coconut, sandalwood, and almond oil removed a few layers of skin. During my massage I was adrift on the sea of nothingness and oblivion, and took a nap subsequently to recover from my stressful day. Afterward, all dressed up, I dined in their flagship restaurant, Kangan, located on the top floor. My Indian dinner of mutton biryani, roti, and samosas was divine. The scenery was washed in soft candlelight and the luminous lights of the city created a fairy tale far below my feet. Fed and nourished, I later surrendered to the soft embrace of the rich cotton bedding.

I woke utterly refreshed and had every intention of getting my city tour arranged with the concierge. Until I saw the rain outside . . . and I learned it was at least two hours one way by taxi to the tourist destinations. They sounded so tempting . . . the Gate of India overlooking the Arabian Sea, Elephanta Island, all the different temples, and street food. Oh, but the comfort and rest of a second day of luxury was too enticing to resist! Mumbai, darling, forgive me for not exploring your tourist treasures. Soon I would be in a mountain hut begging to cope with my first attempt to run 100 miles over five days. Nervous you ask? Hell, yes!

Abode of Snow

IN SANSKRIT "HIM" MEANS snow and "alaya" is a home. The highest mountains with the highest peaks on earth. Giants. Even from their foothills, their range surrounded me like a jagged white necklace crafted by God. The sky was blue and the air was fragrant with the sweet smell of freshly processed tealeaves. Thousands of acres of tea plantations dotted the landscape.

Most of the sixty-three Himalayan 100-mile race participants arrived together in Darjeeling. We were transported to the race headquarters in Mirik nearby in a set of antiquated buses. After a week in India I had faith in the locals' ability to navigate the twisty strings of licorice. I smiled knowingly when I saw the sheer terror in the newcomers' eyes. Aaah. Cows, goats, trucks, pedestrians, cars, buses, more cows (always more cows!) . . . Welcome to India!

Although the locals lived modestly, there was a noticeable absence in the extreme levels of poverty I had seen earlier in the week. I bonded quickly with several of the other racers. Most of us were far from home and some were also rookies like me. Many of the veterans wore the T-shirts from the revered ultra-endurance races across the globe—Bad Water, Mont Blanc, Marathon Des Sables, and Western States.

Later, during the welcome ceremony, the race director handed me my Himalayan 100 T-shirt. How I felt like a newly initiated member to my clan! Small in numbers, we came from afar, willing to test ourselves against the limitations of mind and body. We had distinct reasons for being there, but we all had the overriding goal to finish. Sharing the experience with other crazies was the true treat, I realized much later in the week.

The compassion from the seasoned runners was sincere when they learned it was my first race—short of the two lowly half-marathons I had done in Dallas. Their collective tales of the great races awed me. When I looked across the room, I had never felt so at home among a group of people. Intuitively I knew this would not be my last race. The energy around me was a stiff drink of nonconformity, adventure, and heart.

I also met Tracey that day. Like many other events, an invisible thread connected our destiny. Large was the coincidence when I learned that she used to live a couple of miles from my Dallas neighborhood. We shared the same ob-gyn during the time I was diagnosed with breast cancer, and she lived very near the Texas state capitol in Austin. Our paths crossed in the middle of the Himalayas in India at the start of a 100-mile endurance race. Yeah? Such a fluke.

You are familiar with my toilet paper quirk. There are a few more eccentricities. Not wanting to seem too complex and high maintenance, I have been feeding them to you slowly. I have a thing for pillows. We can safely call it a fetish. Before I turn the light out each night, I shake it several times and smooth the pillowcase until there are no folds or wrinkles. I also replace my pillows every six months when their insides become knotty and my head sinks in between the gaps. I could honestly sleep on a rock if I had a great pillow.

Our accommodation in Mirik, although basic, was adequate. After my Mumbai soiree with luxury and beds from heaven, the mattress was army thin. However, about the pillow. I might as well have slept on a piece of Taj marble. It didn't budge at all. Like the traffic, barking dogs were another incessant Indian trait. I was grateful that my sleeping pills blocked them out for a few hours. Despite modern drugs, no head or neck could stay oblivious to the unyielding thing under my head. Yet still green in roughing it, I lacked a comfy little blow-up pillow. Much smarter these days, I no longer leave home without one! Pillow shopping the next morning was the top planned activity for my last day before tackling huts and such. There was no way I could run 100 bloody miles in the biggest mountains on the planet while sleeping on a crappy pillow!

My REI membership was just a couple of months old. Surprise! Neither North Face nor Patagonia were knocking to sign me up as their outdoor girl doing outdoor adventures and sleeping in outdoor places. I certainly could see myself on the posters. All I lacked was the know-how. Unsuspecting, I was about to start the "Grit Under My Nails" outdoor dirt degree. In India! It excited me that I was about to sleep in my brand-new sleeping bag, carry my pristine race backpack, and spend five days running (probably walking) across the mighty Himalayas! Like a real badass outdoor chick.

Don't judge me too harshly when I confess that I also had my hair done before the race. While strolling through Mirik pillow shopping, the local beauty parlor was open for business. On the spur of the moment I decided to try the "wash and dry" Himalayan style. My sweet hairdresser offered to change my hair color too. Though I'm often spontaneous, that seemed a little bit extreme given the circumstances. The space was tiny with no working plumbing and she promptly stuck a very small heating element in a very large bucket of water. Just having lukewarm water would take hours and I quickly assured her that "cold" was perfectly good. See how fast I'd become outdoor hardy? Back at the hotel with great-looking hair and a pillow that I'd paid Rs.70 ($1.50) for, I happily finished the last of my packing.

We all turned in early for our 6:30 A.M. start of the race. As I rested my head on the softness of my pillow buddy, I knew that the trek to reclaim my freedom from fear was about to begin... with my palms, together, touching my heart... Namaste.

To see a World in a Grain of Sand
And a Heaven in a Wild Flower,
Hold Infinity in the palm of your hand
And Eternity in an hour

—"AUGURIES OF INNOCENCE," WILLIAM BLAKE

One Hundred and Thirty-Two Hours Later

I DIDN'T RECOGNIZE THE stranger who stared back at me in my Delhi hotel bathroom mirror. She didn't care much about the luxurious marble bath being filled or the soft robe and towels nearby. Sinking into the bubbles, the warm water caressed weary bones, loosening the dirt collected from the mountains. She wanted to put her grimy sneakers back on and run down the dimly lit Delhi streets, shouting out to the traffic and street vendors about the sacred place in the clouds that she'd discovered the week before.

After my soak I reacquainted myself with everyday clothes. As I slipped strappy sandals on my worn and blistered feet, I briefly contemplated whether I could get away with flip-flops at the elegant restaurant downstairs awaiting my arrival. It was a night to celebrate. Within the posh limestone lobby of the hotel, my first stop was the lounge bar. Champagne was in order and big was my surprise when

I found Sula Estates on the wine list, made in the true "méthode Champenoise" style near Mumbai. Delicious and crisp, I slowly savored each bubbly sip, sensing that India wanted to raise her glass with me.

My next stop was Paatra, my hotel restaurant, named after the Sanskrit word meaning: 1) a vessel, utensil, receptacle; 2) a deserving person; or 3) a character cast in a dramatic performance. Several delicious courses later while being serenaded by an authentic Indian quartet, I let my mind drift back to our 4:30 A.M. wake-up call the previous Monday morning in Mirik, Day One of the race.

I had to scramble to assemble myself in my race attire and finished packing my two bags—the one that would be transported to the finish line while the other one would accompany me from stage to stage. The race start was an hour and a half away and the bus struggled against the mountain slopes. With sheer drops on both sides of the road, it was the preface to what we had to face later. My stomach was not feeling very good.

The narrow main street of the village was washed in colorful banners and every person, child, and dog (and cow) showed up for the festivity. Following a Tibetan ceremony blessing each of the runners, we were decorated with white prayer scarves. They symbolized purity of intention and celebrated a safe passage. My tears were near as I waited for the start whistle while huddled with the runners at the far back. I had serious concerns about the twenty-four miles ahead while climbing more than 6,000 feet. We were following the cobblestone road to Sandakphu, our camp at the end of stage one. The road was built in 1948 and formed the boundary between India and Nepal.

We were off . . . running through the village streets . . . my heart rate was clocking 160... not good. The first very steep uphill loomed and I sucked oxygen like a smoker trying to get the last drags from a cigarette. Not even past the first mile, my trekking poles were digging into the mountain as I tried to stabilize my heart rate. I could hear my trainer Darvin's voice shouting at me, "Slow down, breathe!" It took some minutes before I gained control over my heart rate. And noticed my surroundings. My English isn't good enough to describe what "breathtaking" really looks like. Imagine after crossing the continental divide in Colorado on I-70 through the Eisenhower Tunnel, the view that stretches before you when you exit. Now imagine the view with mountains almost double in size dwarfing you.

We hugged the Nepalese border and Indian armed border guards were spaced out every kilometer or so. I was soon accustomed to see the guards with AK-47s beside the trail. With limited English, they willingly posed for photos and cheered us on our way. The race markers were in kilometers and the simple math to convert to miles escaped me. Local volunteers manned the aid stations that were stocked with water, bananas, boiled potatoes, and salt and sugar cookies.

Many villagers ambled along, mostly in worn sandals or rain boots, effortlessly balancing huge loads on their backs. The cobblestones mercilessly dug into my feet. I had to concentrate all my focus not to twist an ankle on the uneven ground. Around Mile Ten the terrain leveled out a little and snaked through picturesque bamboo forests and streams. I had the audacity to start to run. The bamboo gently brushed against me as I passed, touching me lovingly with their thin, feathery leaves. Yeah! I could do this race!

Single since the start, I was too slow for the faster runners and slightly faster than the slowest. My iPod happily turned out the songs from my playlist. Right after the aid station at Mile Fourteen my torture kicked into high gear. How could anything be this steep! Switchback after switchback, straight into the sky, the road stretched ahead with no end. The mountains were covered in their thick afternoon coats, and their mist quickly enveloped me. Several layers of clothes did not keep out their reach. Cold and damp, my bones craved warmth while my mind told them to keep moving.

"This is not possible!" I silently screamed at the mountains. Supertramp's "The Logical Song" was my iPod shuffle pick and I listened to the timeless lyrics about wanting someone to tell me who I am. I could not control the tears streaming down my face. Shaking and shivering somewhere in the Himalayas, I acknowledged what a mess everything had become. My battlefield was drawn between the rivers of worthiness and survival. On the one side I was deathly afraid that my breath would be stolen from me too early. On the other side my intense struggle to prove that I was worthy to be cherished for the wild, untamed, and one-of-a-kind creature I was.

I had to get off this mountain before dark. Exhausted, I pushed upward and onward, barely registering the haunting beauty of my surroundings. When I approached the last 100 meters I was greeted by some of my race buddies. They were waiting to escort me home. I stumbled across the finish line and doubled over as sobs raked me apart. Nine hours had passed since the start. I had nothing left to give and had never felt so naked and aware of my own raw self.

The staff offered me a bucket of hot water for washing but with the outside temperatures near freezing, I decided that my sweat could stay put. My priorities were hot soup and warm, dry clothes.

I had just enough energy to unroll my down sleeping bag and pad. Luckily, the pillow from Mirik had also made it to camp. My bones, together with a tired mind, snuggled easily inside the cozy comfort.

Titans Awake!

FOUR A.M. WAKE-UP CALL . . . I reluctantly unwrapped myself from my snug down cocoon and braved the biting cold of Day Two. My joints were stiff and I ached all over. But how often do you get to see daybreak and the sunrise over Mt. Everest? The early morning sky was crystal clear and still cloaked in midnight black. Without any obstacles blocking my view, eternity stretched out in front of me and all I had to do was reach out and grasp it. My troubles and throbbing muscles seemed small against the backdrop of such holiness.

I silently watched black transformed to indigo. Mother Nature held her breath with me as dawn was about to be cracked wide open. The sun announced its imminent arrival with just a thin ribbon of fiery orange playing a cheeky peek-a-boo with the horizon. The mountain peaks were still dark silhouettes and patiently awaited their tender morning kiss by the first rays. I could feel God present in the splendor in front of me. A profound sense of internal peace and solace slowly soaked into my being and eased out the pain from Day One.

Triumphantly the sun arrived and washed creation in shades of pink, crimson, and orange. The snowy peaks burned like uncontrolled bush fires! The great ones revealed their glory to me one by one—Mount Everest, Lhotse, Makalu, and Kanchenjunga—larger-than-life natural wonders commanding the horizon! I watched in silent awe and was curious what it would be like to reach their summits. Through photographs I try to capture moments like this, but ultimately you must make the journey to grasp its magnificence. Freshly anointed with the miracle of my surroundings, I was unafraid of the twenty miles ahead.

Ten miles out and back. Each downhill out was the uphill struggle back. The vistas were spectacular and the mountain peaks flirted for my attention. Sticking to my sensible plan for Day Two, I walked to the turnaround aid station dead last. Maybe it was the mountain deities who decided to intervene . . . maybe it was the runner hiding somewhere inside me . . . maybe I was just pissed off being last . . . on the way back I picked up my feet and ran. For real. My trekking poles became extensions of my arms and turned me into a four-legged mountain gazelle. Sure-footed and confident over the uneven terrain, I overtook several runners. Their surprise was as great as mine at my speed and agility!

What a glorious day! The Himalayas were a remarkable place to practice the fine art of running! Kanchenjunga personally rewarded me at sunset and briefly revealed its radiant summit from behind the spun cotton candy clouds ablaze as night was falling. That night with palms together, my "Namaste" was filled with appreciation for the infinite blessings bestowed upon me.

Spilling Secrets

ON THE EVE OF Day Three, it was our last night at Sandakphu at almost 13,000 feet, and the 6,000-foot descent awaited us in the morning. I would miss our simple huts in the sky and the company of my splendid mountains. By my side they silently witnessed my agony and joy on their ridges, peaks, and foothills. They tested my tolerance with their steep cobblestones, chilled me with their foggy breaths, and awarded me with their pageantry. Akin to family, we were connected. My therapist shares your concern about the rate at which I adopt trees, whale sharks, leopards, mountains, volcanoes, etc. At least I'm not the hermit dwelling with ten cats and dogs at the end of a farm road. I also have yet to give any of these unusual companions names. Except of course for my horse, Caston, but he was more than family.

Having been warned that bad weather could move in, making the way down very treacherous, my confidence slipped a little from the pedestal of the previous day. Initially it was a blast. The first few miles were another out and back. It allowed me to intercept many of my newfound friends. The front-runners passed by me in full flight, their only mission to reach the finish first. Countless hugs later from my fellow racers, I wanted to rename the ridge "Via Amigos." How quickly we cut through the crap when united by hurting muscles, blistered feet, painful injuries, and the sheer will to continue. In such a setting pretense held no weight and everyone became intimate friends fast.

Shortly after my descent into the valley, a sharp pain in my left knee stopped me in my tracks. Ugh! All I could do was wrap it as best I could with the compression bandage I had stuffed in my belt. I had little practice running (or walking) with pain and my bravado vaporized. From nowhere my running friend Giorgio from Italy appeared, offering to escort me as I hobbled down the steep mountainside. His willingness to stay with me was like a warm bowl of comforting homemade minestrone with fresh bread and grated Parmigiano-Reggiano cheese. Our reflective conversations down the mountains about love, connection, and the meaning of it all caused me much pause.

Maybe it was because my physical pain eclipsed the hurt in my heart. Maybe by the end of Day Three the effort to keep the rust and ruin from shining through was just too much. Maybe it was because Giorgio's compassion embraced me in kindness when I arrived at the intersection that an endurance race brings you to—quit or tolerate suffering. But maybe it was just time to share the story of a shredded letter whose torn pieces matched my frayed insides.

In the shadow of Mt. Everest I shared with Giorgio who my father could be according to the revelation in Mother's last letter. He was a sympathetic listener, and it was easy to tell him about the cruel game she had played for so many years. I told him about Gert, how he was the wind that gently steered my sails along a plotted course I could never see. It made such sense. Why would anybody agree to take in someone's kid? Unless she was your daughter.

But what if in this letter to me she had lied once again? What if her perverse mind plotted a quicksand I could not escape? I had held on to her final confession since 1995 without finding the courage to pursue the truth. Was Gert really my father? Her version of events had suggested that she'd had an affair with him as a younger woman. By now I had been sitting on her final revelation for years like a brooding hen on some unfertile eggs, unable to decide what to do next.

Late into his eighties, Gert had died in 1996, a year after I'd received her letter. By then his mind was feeble, and there was no point in having the conversation to find out the truth. In the years following his death I hesitated to share the possibility with other members of my Makwassie family. The desire to know the truth and the fear to know the truth burned side by side. My own inertia left me paralyzed.

I had always considered it less painful to remain unsure than to fully comprehend the possible depth of her deception. She died somewhere around 2008, although it's unclear exactly how, when, and where. The location of her grave is as big a mystery as what transpired with her since the day I left South Africa in 1990. I had no contact with my half-siblings either. William and Tienie shared the news of her death after they found out about it thirdhand. At the same time William learned that my half-brother had been killed in an armed robbery while working as a security guard.

Her death found me indifferent. I had never envisioned mending our differences. Although I heard her heartbeat for nine months from the inside, we were strangers to each other. As a mother myself to my own two beloved children, I just accept that I never had a real mother. Our flaw resided in our inability to unconditionally accept each other for who we were. As a youngster, from a place of complete dread and an absence of trust, I'd built a fortress around myself and lacked the courage to ever let her in.

Per Angusta Ad Augusta

I CAN SUM UP the rest of Day Three in a few simple words: *In your face, sucker!* In sections, rough wooden steps guided us downward and the lush foliage created a dense green curtain around us. Multicolored wildflowers and Himalaya prayer flags dotted the landscape. They had been a constant reminder of the Buddhist influence on this part of India. I learned that their colors of blue, white, red, green, and yellow represented the elements: sky/space, air/wind, fire, water, and earth. I was optimistic that the mantras and prayers for longevity and good fortune inscribed upon them held blessings for me to borrow from.

Abruptly the forest surrendered to the river and Giorgio and I were treated to white water tumbling over boulders and rushing down riverbeds. Daylight faded fast as we crossed over its bridge. A few miles later I reached the finish line after eleven and a half hours. Emotionally and physically spent, my signature on the race sheet was a flat line. Done. Done. And done.

Rimbik Lodge held the promise of a warm shower, hot food, a cold beer, flushing toilets, and a softer bed. It did score on two out of the five (the food was great and the beer ample). Our rooms were as basic as the huts in the mountains and faced with another night of baby wipes, I submissively unrolled my sleeping bag and pad.

In the company of my mountain family, we celebrated our fortunes of Day Three over Kingfisher Indian beer while carb-loading. I had never eaten rice, pasta, bread, and noodles with some chicken and a touch of veggies, all on the same plate! Our GPS readings placed the day at thirty-three miles and as I snuggled into the soft down comfort of my sleeping bag, I briefly worried about the next day's half marathon.

My feet stayed miraculously blister free but my hands were not so lucky. The many hours of gripping my trekking poles for balance and strength had left bleeding wounds. Most of Day Four was on downhill asphalt roads while meandering through charming villages. Soon after the start, my tightly bandaged knee gave out and I knew I was in for a thirteen-mile downward shuffle. My roommate Sue and friend Tracey from Austin were my Good Samaritans. Together we walked the distance in 3.5 hours and coined the label "Sisterhood of Mountain Travelers." I had time to tell Tracey in much detail all about dense breast tissue and my effort underway to pass a bill to educate women and potentially save lives. Little did I know how much her invitation to stay with her in Austin as often as needed would become my aid station there.

Crossing the finish line was my only objective and success for me was not about my final placement among the other participants. I could never have imagined how hard these days would be, nor foreseen how extraordinary the experience, how priceless the friendships I would forge, and how valuable the memories that were mine to keep.

Day Five. The bitch from hell whose name I have tried to ignore ever since. Seventeen miles and pain stood between defeat or victory. Stuffed with enough pills to open a pharma road stand, my plan was simple: Walk it, crawl it, keep moving forward and make it. Feel the pain but don't surrender to it. Six miles up and eleven miles down.

The end.

My company was mountain streams and waterfalls that harmonized their song and gently conveyed their music. Tall trees reminiscent of the redwoods in Northern California lined the snaky and twisting road like soldiers silently watching over my measured progress. The lush green foliage, filled with ferns, flowers, and the many shrubs with no names spilled over the roads. An abundant display of all of nature's countless shades of green delighted me—emerald, olive, lime, jade, sea, and bottle green. The friendly "Namaste" from the locals was bittersweet. My time here was ending.

My road to the finish line was "Redemption Way." Fate steered me to this race when I had little fight left in me. In the years leading up to my cancer diagnosis I had detoured from resilience, courage, and endurance—the skills I had learned so well when I was young. I had lost my way. During the race I became reacquainted with strength, perseverance, and the will not to quit. By the end of 2009 God strong-armed me up this cliff edge before mercilessly pushing me off, knowing that I would rediscover my grit in flight.

I slowly ran the final fifty meters, and when I broke the tape as the last runner for Day Five my exuberance overflowed. Washed in the joy of reaching my goal, I sensed that I had changed the course of my very being. My playbook no longer had any lines. By nearly drowning myself I learned how solid my stroke was. I understood what Augustine meant about immortality starting with living a life worth remembering.

Aftershock

I N DELHI I TOOK my finisher trophy with me to my celebratory dinner at Paatra. I basked in the warm glow of ending #47 out of sixty-three runners. Although I was fully willing to be last, it tasted so sweet to learn that I was not. I had to pinch myself a few times to ensure that I was not trapped in a fantasy. I really had completed a 100-mile ultra-extreme endurance race at 13,000 feet over five days in the mightiest mountains known to man.

But there was another race in progress and its outcome was much more imperative than the Himalayan 100 could ever be. The United States general elections of 2010 unfolded upstairs on my laptop and the 11.5-hour time difference made it still very early in Dallas. The voting polls had only been open a few hours when I turned the light out to try to sleep some before the results were announced.

While I trained for the race during the summer and fall of 2010, my state congressman, Allen Vaught, met with many doctors across Texas from UT Southwestern, Baylor Medical Center, and the Paul L. Foster School of Medicine in El Paso to the M.D. Anderson Cancer Center in Houston. He sought their support for legislation he planned to introduce during the 2011 Texas legislative session. The bill would require FDA-approved mammogram facilities to inform women about dense breast tissue and the limitations of a mammogram detecting a tumor in dense breasts. The legislation would also ensure that at-risk women had access to supplemental screening.

I had one more week left in India and the next morning, just before I left for the airport to catch my flight to Varanasi, I was almost too anxious to log on to my computer. Vaught, a moderate Democrat, had served two terms and his challenger was a newcomer Tea Party Republican. I was shocked when I saw the final results. Vaught had lost the reelection. I was speechless. Devastated. Angry. Unspeakably disappointed. Bloody angry. Dumbstruck. Crushed. Nooooooooo!

Darn it! I didn't have a Plan B. He had to win. That was the plan! The bottom dropped out of my stomach and I thought I was going to vomit. My ears were ringing and I could see little black spots in front of me. I had to sit down on the bed to prevent myself from falling. How could chance play this sick trick on me after all that had happened? It wasn't possible that my aspiration to save a few lives had become a distant mirage fading fast into obscurity. Over the past twenty-four hours I had caught the thermals, soared, but then crashed into pieces.

In a perverse way I was back on the foggy mountain of Day One. Lost and cold.

I wanted to crawl into a ball, find a cave, and hibernate for the winter. Instead I had already planned to spend my last few days in India with my oncologist surgeon's family in Varanasi. Situated on the banks of the Ganges, it was the sacred city to both the Buddhists and Hindus and one of the holiest places of all pilgrimages. I decided to pack away my grave disappointment about the election and enjoy my final days in India as best I could.

Silk and Spice and Everything Nice

THE FIRST EVENING IN Varanasi introduced me to the finest of traffic jams. "Stuck" was a concept we could contemplate, but unless you were squeezed tightly between a large rock and a very hard place, you could not be as trapped as we were. I counted the eyelashes of the people who were flattened against our car windows. In the utter chaos people were skin to skin, metal to metal, metal to flesh, and spike to metal. Let's not forget the cows, dogs, goats, donkeys, or the relentless honking. The swelling waves of my claustrophobia rushed over me and I had to resist the urge to climb onto the roof of our car.

India's street energy pulsed with the intensity of its own life force. While spending time in it, I felt as if I stuck my fingers in its outlet and could absorb some of it. It was filled with vendors on wheeled carts selling everything and anything: sugarcane, bicycles, potatoes, plants, pots and pans, boxes, silk, religious relics, food, shoes, and marigold flowers to take to temple. It was like a giant mobile Super Target split into little pieces, continuously in motion and on wheels. Among the anarchy the pedestrian's struggle on foot was a battle of courage, guts, and determination.

Around every corner and down every street, people were on the move, and their haste reminded me of a very intricate dance routine. I became part of their dance every time I crossed a street. I danced an Indian tango with them and the rest of the madness: a very slow, seductive, and dangerous routine of pauses, pivots, and turns in a very close embrace, trying my best to survive each crossing.

My last day in India. I greeted the sun as it debuted over the Ganges, the holy river for the Hindus. I wore my exquisitely gifted sari from my hosts when twilight painted the new day in pale blue ambient light just before the first rays of the sun washed the temples and shrines in a golden hue along the river. I watched as thousands of people bathed in the blessed waters, envisioning shedding my own robes and baggage that easily and stepping into my own waters of reverence.

Varanasi's spirit echoed loudly within me. As I stood under the tree in Sarnath where Buddha delivered his first sermon, I desired to be touched by my own enlightenment. I longed for the same peace I felt from the orange-clad monks at the monasteries I visited. But I understood it was a journey and I had just launched mine. Much work was left to craft the authentic person I aspired to become.

India seduced me bit by bit and unhurriedly waited for me to fall for its intoxicating offerings. It was as if it knew it would simply be a matter of time before I succumbed and grasped the pull of its 5,000-year-old soul. Initially it overwhelmed me with its hardships. It revealed to me the raw center of its pain and the bleak existence of so many of its people. The images of the outcast and destitute bombarded me with their cries until my mind was numb. I felt such sadness for the lost and lonely who called the streets their home.

In stark contrast it also showered me with the wealth of its treasures. The greatness of its past was reflected in the perfection of the translucent marble of the Taj Mahal. I became connected with the great Himalayas, formed when India ruptured from Africa and slammed into Asia millions of years ago. The secret of India's charm may rest in the fact that it was also part of Africa eons before. Maybe the attraction was forged at our foundation as I recognized similar extremes within me.

I boarded my plane back to Dallas, my arms and hands elaborately henna-tattooed in the timeless art of Mehndi. The lotus flower designs wrapped around my wrists and palms and entwined my fingers, signifying my own awakening from within. I made peace with the fact that my ambition to change the standard of care for women with dense breast tissue might have to be shelved, barring mythical intervention. I still had complete faith that my cancer had a purpose. I would just have to let each day reveal what that looked like. Governor Perry would simply have to sign a law during the next session that neither he nor anybody in Austin had any knowledge about. Although maybe not religious in the traditional sense, I undoubtedly believed in miracles. C'mon, divine ones, pay attention!

There is special providence in the fall of a sparrow. If it be now, 'tis not to come; if it be not to come, it will be now; if it be not now, yet it will come—the readiness is all. Since no man, of aught he leaves, knows what is't to leave betimes? Let be.

—SHAKESPEARE, *HAMLET*, ACT 5, SCENE 2

Charging Hell with a Bucket of Ice Water

I SAT ON A bench inside the Texas capitol in Austin trying to interpret the map that showed the different legislative offices. I might as well have been studying an ancient treasure map in Greek. I felt quite teary and had no doubt that if I was on a reality game show I would be voted off. The capitol was a maze, and I had no foggy idea how to locate the representatives and senators' offices where I was supposed to be in less than ten minutes.

Just hours before, on a very crisp Tuesday morning in late January 2011, I had my first introduction with this iconic Texas landmark. The pale pink granite of the capitol was washed in the warm rays of the early morning sun. Atop the dome Lady Liberty silently observed my approach and I felt sure that the same thought had crossed both our minds: "What the heck is *she* doing here?"

My stomach was a tight knot of nerves. It was a complete miracle for me to be in Austin. I had given up expectations that anything could be accomplished after Vaught lost his reelection bid in November. But the mysterious twists and turns of my cancer train were not slowing down. A Texas representative from Houston ended up hiring Vaught's legislative director who then presented my bill to her new boss, who also happened to be firmly committed to women's health issues. Suddenly we had a real bill to pass! My latest ally was in her second term, and I easily promised her my full support to help in any way possible.

I found myself in Austin at the start of the New Year because my dense breast tissue bill named "Henda's Law" was being filed in the 82nd legislative session in the state of Texas's house and senate. The sponsored senator and state representative had invited me to attend what was for them a routine activity, whereas for me it had altered my world's spin.

Mentally putting on my big girl panties, I got up from the bench, stepped through the capitol building's wooden doors, and went into the rotunda. Surrounded by portraits of the past presidents of the Republic of Texas and the past governors of the state of Texas, the enormity of the moment caught me by surprise. September 2003's memory was still fresh when I took the oath to become an American citizen and recited my first Pledge of Allegiance.

Eight short years later I was now witness to a bill carrying my name being filed at the Texas state capitol to help women fight breast cancer. Geez, Louise. Not sure who did the choosing here as I had neither a hat nor cattle to fit into this party.

"Breathe, just breathe," I kept repeating to myself. "And please don't cry . . . or throw up!" My tears had a mind of their own and forced themselves past all the naysayers. It had been less than two years since I was knocked sideways by cancer. I had a strange sense that I stood exactly where I was supposed to be at that moment. Without sounding corny, I felt inherently responsible to help other women avoid a late diagnosis.

Sigh. India had certainly sorted some of my "psychological issues" regarding my heart but I was still a nutcase at large. Not to worry. I'm better these days, although I cry even easier! But don't you agree that it seemed predetermined? Like cancer handpicked me? I think the plan always was to transport me from South Africa to Austin. Anyway, it makes me feel better thinking that the whole C-thing was part of a higher purpose.

I finally located the senator's office. He was one of the senior members, a longtime legislator and a Democrat. His stern farewell message matched his imposing stature as he towered over me. "Little girl, although I filed the senate bill, it's up to you to garner bipartisan support to get it passed!"

Sufficiently warned, my second stop was the capitol gift store to buy the 2011 legislature handbook. Inside were all the senators and representatives' names listed, their office locations, as well as their legislative directors and aides. I also bought a striking Texas star bracelet with ten vermeil gold stars linked together. It was for good luck. My promise? I would not take it off until the bill had passed.

The size of the capitol from the outside is completely misleading, as half of it is underground. Juggling the advice in the handbook and the information on my map was like trying to scale a massive mountain in flip-flops. Paging through the handbook, I realized I had no idea how to implement the advice from my fall reading, *The Midwest Academy*. On a whim I decided to initially target the state representatives from the North Texas area, but my attempts to speak to anybody misfired. I never made it past the secretaries safeguarding their domains. I soon found myself on another bench ready to shed more tears. I could hear Mandela whisper, "Courage is not the absence of fear, but the triumph over it. The brave man is not he who does not feel afraid, but he who conquers that fear." I knew he would advise me to implement a better plan than my current Wonderful World of Waterworks. But until then I felt like a complete crying loser.

Searching for a Whisper in a Whirlwind

FORTUNATELY, MY FRIEND TRACEY lived nearby and just like so much else, meeting her in India during the Himalayan 100 race had proved to be no coincidence. She was my hut mate on the race at 13,000 feet and my steadfast companion on the painful Day Four when finishing seemed unlikely. I was equally bruised and battered after my first day as a lobbyist when I arrived on her doorstep in Austin. Having a friend that evening was like a cold glass of lemonade on a blazing Texas summer day. Staying with her would be a godsend in the weeks and months to come, along with her support, encouragement, and friendship.

The next morning, armed with photocopies of the bill and dressed in a dark pink dress given to me by Tracey, I was invigorated to try once more. I almost felt like waving to Lady Liberty this time as I walked up to the daunting pink granite structure. Almost immediately I ran into an aide for a very senior house representative. He was familiar with my efforts, thanks to our mutual lobbyist friend, Douglas. I told him about my struggles to get my foot in the door the day before, and he gave some advice that became one of the jewels inside my Austin war chest. He coached me to hand out something tangible that would stand out on desks brimming over with paperwork from the thousands of bills filed each session. Additionally, he counseled me to have a very short, memorable summary of the bill as part of my handout with the "what" and "why" very prominently displayed. His parting suggestion was to have a pitch-perfect elevator speech at the ready.

I decided to spend the rest of that day just getting lost inside the maze. It was like a scavenger hunt. I randomly picked an office from my handbook and tried to find it without walking in too many circles. Once I figured out that the letters N, S, W, or E in front of the room numbers represented directions on a compass, I was in good shape. And here you thought I joked about my sincere failure at understanding directions!

When I left the capitol at the end of the day, I blew a kiss to my statue friend perched high above. Bravely, young leaves had burst early from their sleepy cocoon to defy the late winter setting. The air smelled of earth and freshness, and I envisioned bottling its distinct fragrance. It was my kind of season. I could not help but sense a resurgence of hope that maybe my efforts would not be a complete fiasco.

Driving north back home to Dallas, I had no idea how many times I would undertake this same 400-mile round trip to the state house in the coming months. My first introduction to the reality of politics felt like an old-school hazing. It dawned on me that instead of trying to become a politician, I should stick with what I was familiar with. Sales. I was no politician and had no skill passing a law. But I knew how to sell. I had been a top residential real estate expert selling a lot of high-end homes. By the time I pulled into my driveway that evening it was suddenly so clear—passing this bill would require me to perform the best sales job ever!

Anticipating that I would be back in Austin very soon, I had little time to get professionally made handouts, so I went the homemade route. I had learned something else from trying to get past the secretaries. Not only is "dense breast tissue" a tongue twister, but people's eyes quickly glazed over. The regular response of "Wait, what?" after my elevator speech was almost comical. There was never enough time to explain what the three words meant. The perfect "show" was a picture of my own mammogram hiding a four-centimeter tumor. Almost poetically, just prior to my breast surgery in 2009, the radiologist had implanted a very tiny titanium ribbon to mark my tumor location—an image that showed up clearly on my mammogram. Luck continued to be my partner, as my local Office Depot had stacks of "Komen" pink folders with the universally recognized pink ribbon embellished on the front. I bought every single one I could locate from all the area stores.

I made more than 150 folders with a one-page summary of the bill, compelling breast cancer facts, my tumor-hiding mammogram side by side with a mammogram showing how easy it is to spot a tumor in a fatty un-dense breast, and a drawing of a ruler displaying how big 4cm is. Just in case people didn't know it was the diameter of a golf ball. At the time I was very active in my local Komen for the

Cure affiliate and was profoundly grateful when the Texas affiliates wrote a letter in support of the bill. It emphasized the importance of informing women about dense breast tissue. Both the Komen letter and a local magazine article about my story with pictures of my kids completed my handouts. I signed each cover letter "Thank You, Henda" with a fuchsia marker.

Leveraging the widespread association between breast cancer and pink, I decided that my marching uniforms for Austin would be dresses and jackets in all shades of pink. A quick stop at the local mall instantly expanded my wardrobe. It was show time! I was ready to show and share the story and picture of my right boob with every person I could get in front of—whether a parking attendant, aide, senator, representative, lobbyist, or assistant.

One-Legged at a Butt-Kicking Convention

AS YOU ARE BY now a specialist in breast density, let's kick up the curriculum. Get ready for the bull-dust class about Texas politics. One cannot make this stuff up! Hang with me for the next few pages because by the end, we can start a contract lobbyist firm specializing in fertilizer and elephant dung (a.k.a. total BS!).

The bill had two components. Part one informed and educated women about their breast density and the benefits of supplemental screening. Part two required insurance carriers to cover supplemental screening for women with dense breasts as part of their annual wellness exams. There was about a zero chance of passing the insurance part in a Republican-controlled house and senate with a conservative governor at the wheel. But the information and education part had a chance and was known as House Bill 834 (HB-834).

I also received a crash course on the timeline of passing bills and all the committees and hearings it had to successfully navigate in order to land on the governor's desk for signature. Thousands of bills die on the vine during each session, meaning they never make it to the governor before the 140 days of the regular legislative session runs out. In this case that crucial date was May 30, 2011.

In early March we filed a second bill in the house, HB-2102. It contained only the insurance portion to separate it from the more promising HB-834. Working two bills with their own timelines necessitated double the testifying and lobbying. I stuffed additional information inside my pink folders to clearly communicate the differences between the two and added a legend to keep all the numbers and nuances straight. When the session opened I thought I could dance quite well. Right. Let's take some more dance lessons! And while at it, let me learn to speak Texan real good, as I had no daylight to burn.

The best strategy was to defer to the professional lobbyists and seasoned political staff members, learning from them how to navigate the storm waters of Texas politics. I quickly discovered that the capitol cafeteria was a powerful place to linger with the intention of running into key people. My tactics paid off when some of the various allies I had made over repeated visits would text me to "show up" in the cafeteria whenever a critical aide or lobbyist had been spotted buying lunch. I had perfected my message and could flawlessly deliver the sound bites in less than two minutes. I rattled off my story over and over with no loss of enthusiasm all spring. It was draining, the reliving and retelling of those dark days after my cancer diagnosis to politicians' staff who were jaded by a system that had little room and even less time for a novice like me.

My fiercest supporter remained my *Midwest Academy* friend and mentor from the Texas Hold 'Em poker game. Douglas wasn't kidding when he assured me that I would need every special interest group to be either in favor of or at least not opposing the bills. Once again drawing on my background in sales and gut instinct, I tried to decipher which staff members for each representative and senator were the decision makers on what reached their boss's desk and got his or her attention. My friend made many introductory calls on my behalf, and without his guidance I would have had a very slim chance of succeeding. That said, he did withhold some essential information. He failed to tell me that the success of most bills also hinged on the elbow twisting, schmoozing, and lobbying during the off year between legislative sessions. A bill filed two weeks into the current session stood a less-than-zero chance of making it beyond filed status. He also didn't let me in on the secret of how "big money" rules Texas politics. With a state as large as Texas, running for office requires buckets of money like a federal campaign. Special interests are king, and I had no idea that Texas politics were in the same league as New York and California as far as complexity.

By the end of the 140 days of the 82nd Texas legislature on May 30, I would have earned the equivalent of a bachelor's degree in political science. The difference was that I earned it on the ground in combat instead of from books in a classroom. It was a war of attrition as I fought not with superior skill or strength, but instead with an unwavering faith in what was right. Not to mention clever resource management.

Since the first breast density law in the United States passed in Connecticut in 2009, a small army of seven women had evolved, all fighting on our individual state fronts. In addition to Texas, similar efforts by women like me were underway in Florida, Virginia, California, New York, and Missouri. We were all survivors of a later-stage diagnosis, our tumors were all undetected by mammograms, and we all had dense breast tissue. I felt incredible pressure to deliver the goods in a large, very red state. If Texas could pass a density bill, other states would leverage the momentum and the density snowball would get rolling.

For a bill to be signed by the governor and become law in Texas, it must pass with a majority vote in the house and senate. As both bills worked their way through the house, I would often get calls in Dallas at 7:00 A.M. from a staff member to come down to Austin to testify. Armed with my folders and always wearing a pretty pink dress, I would drop everything in Dallas for the three-hour drive to the capitol.

Testifying in front of the different house committees for more than a month was nerve-racking. I wrote out my testimony to maximize the six to eight minutes allocated to ensure that I didn't miss vital points. This was one time I was not depending on my ability to improvise, and I practiced my message until it evolved into a smooth delivery of why this legislation was necessary. Taking my place behind the podium in the different committee chambers, I was aware of a small red light blinking when I had neared my time. Each committee member had the chance to ask me follow-up questions. My outward calm belied my insides of twisted rubber bands ready to snap.

Before and after testifying I continued meandering the halls and handing out my pink folders to anybody in sight. Luck was often looking out for me. One time I walked in on the birthday party of a senior Democrat who also happened to be a breast cancer survivor. After telling her my story I could count on her vote! Good fortune was also on my team on another occasion when a veteran aide pulled me aside, tore off a piece of paper from her notebook, and wrote down about thirty names. She advised me to focus my efforts on them and their staff members, deeming them the real bigwigs at the capitol. I also had a short list of the main special interest lobbyists to target. The bill stood no chance without their support.

I was humbled by the large number of people I talked to who were touched by cancer, whether personally or through their family and friends. Cancer was the common thread we shared, and it crossed all party lines and demographics.

Possum Pie for Dinner

I HAVE A FRIEND who says that a big sky opens our mind. Since transplanting myself to Texas the spectacular display of such a sky has rarely failed to render me speechless—whether a sunrise or sunset, the moon debuting, or white clouds dancing across its great expanse. After I left the capitol for Dallas I was often treated to an extraordinary sunset that made me feel like a VIP guest at the sun's farewell performance. It teased me with its reluctance to drop out of sight and rewarded me with several encores before taking a last bow. Hanging like a fireball in the west and streaking flares across the sky in Morse code, it brilliantly colored the wide-open spaces of nightfall in crimson.

I exhaled as I drove, letting go of more of the tension knotted in every corner of my being with each mile I clocked. My mind had permission to remove its shoes and wiggle itself loose from the confines I had stuck myself in to stay on message with all the players at the capitol. Nature's powerful presence on those nights was my private comfort guide. It assured me that the detours, twists, and turns were all part of it. As a train lover I recognized that it was never about the journey or the destination; it was choosing to board the train. I felt I was on a runaway express speeding down a steep mountain.

The soothing qualities of food always play a valuable part in my experiences, and the treks back and forth to Austin were no different. That spring and early summer I discovered roasted marrowbones from Durham, Wyoming, and the best fattoush salad this side of Lebanon. Even the Capitol Grill surprised me with fresh mozzarella and pesto on nutty bread. Left over from my radiation days, finding great Texas BBQ is still a prized pursuit, and I never miss an opportunity to unearth the next best brisket, ribs, and coleslaw.

Driving home from Austin, I almost always stopped at a barbecue joint near I-35 to sample their smoked meat and side dish specialties. I avoided the big chains and instead sought out the smaller mom & pop spots. Dressed in my pink ensemble and heels, I was used to being stared at as the drop-in alien. I once stopped near Abbott, Texas, (population 356), but it was not my lucky day because the slaw was out, the brisket cold, and the sauce neither smoky nor sweet. While enjoying some decent barbecue beans and ribs, I suddenly sensed that I was no longer alone and felt two piercing eyes staring at me. After scanning the crowd my gaze shifted down to the ground beneath my dinner table and I came eye to eye with a sizable possum! I assumed that he had come for dinner as well, perhaps sensing how out of place we both were. As I didn't speak Possum, our silent conversation was a little limited, the exchange brief, and I never did get his recommendations for better brisket stops nearby. On my way out I mentioned to the server about the possum looking for scraps and was met with an effusive, "Hell, Honey! And you did not scream?" I just smiled, wanting to assure her that it takes politicians, not possums, to make me cry.

Hauling Ass

By early May I was exhausted by lobbying in Austin and I welcomed the distraction of settling an old score. Let's revisit my ICU room-with-a-view in Arequipa back in dreadful 2009. When my friggin' heart had trouble keeping a beat! I bargained with El Misti's summit then to give me a shot standing on its 19,100-foot top . . . alive. As it turned out an unexpected opportunity presented itself to me to accompany my father-in-law to the land of his birth and my phantom city since August 2009. Although the Himalayan 100 had managed to corral some of my crazies, I welcomed the chance to leave a few more behind on an active volcano.

I met with my hired guide, Jose, and between his English and my Spanish, it appeared that we would be a good team. He warned me that the night temperatures would drop to minus-something and with the wind, it would be "very cold." We planned to climb to base camp the first day and then start the trek for the summit at 2:00 A.M. the following morning. The descent would be very quick and I would be back in Arequipa by the end of the day if all went per our plan.

I was amazed at the speed our Sherpa could maintain with his backpack and mine strung on top. His agility and strength was astounding, and I was embarrassed by how much my ten-pound daypack strained my own progress. The bottom part of the mountain was an ocean of black sand dunes. With each step my shoes sunk further into the soft fine powder that stuck to my skin like iridescent black dust.

Base camp was at 13,500 feet and marked by a stack of rocks to shield us from the brutal wind on the mountain face. Between Jose the guide and David the Sherpa, our tents went up quickly. With limited camping expertise, I was grateful that others oversaw my well-being. Dusk was upon us when I joined the boys in the "dinner" tent to test the strength of my Spanish. By now I was wearing two pairs of thermal underwear, ski pants, a thermal top, a fleece, a thick down jacket, a hat, and gloves. Dinner consisted of bread, canned spaghetti, and a packet of chicken soup. I had always followed the mantra "when in Rome" and very soon I was discussing the upcoming Peruvian elections with my two dinner companions—in Spanish! I'm not sure who was more amazed! It was a little like playing charades where I used my limited vocabulary to describe what I wanted to say and then either Jose or David would chime in with the missing words. Two hours later we chatted like old friends over cups of steaming hot chocolate and tea.

The brilliance of the night sky away from city lights has always left me in awe. That night God treated me to an incomparable masterpiece where the stars were dazzling diamonds on rich black velvet. I could wrap my hands around the Milky Way and hold the stars close to my beating heart. Above me the Southern Cross shined brightly, a vivid beacon to remind me that I could always find my way home. But 2:00 A.M. arrived far too soon. After hot tea and bread, the trek to the top began. In single file, our headlamps pierced the night to light our way. Soon my fingers were frozen—why did I bring my running gloves instead of my ski gloves? Hours later I was still fixated on my freezing cold hands. My guide, Jose, sensed my misery and graciously offered his. Knowing that mine would never warm his, I reluctantly declined.

Dawn arrived and I could finally grasp the expanse of the surreal moonscape surrounding us this high up, as well as the tremendous slope we were up against. We were the only three people summiting the volcano that day, and we'd left our emergency oxygen tanks far below at base camp. My anxiety ran like a Kentucky Derby winner down the stretch. This headline kept playing in my head: "Breast Cancer Survivor Tragically Dies of Heart Attack on Active Volcano." Practicing the fine art of breathing while not surrendering to sheer panic, I tried to focus on dawn. The sun was target shooting its first round of orange bullets across the sci-fi-like landscape. Alien and barren, I felt a connection with the desolate isolation of our surroundings.

Hour after hour I also watched my oxygen saturation plummet on my oximeter. Having followed the advice of my doctor friends, I had taken Diamox for six days to combat altitude sickness. I was grateful for any additional O_2 floating in my blood. With labored breath and tired legs, each step became harder. The mountain was slowly pulling ahead as the favorite to win the day. But my heart rate was stable in the nineties, and my faith in its continued long-term operation was slowly growing.

The boys paced with me as we climbed higher and higher, but our stops became more frequent. Jose kept us moving and I was grateful for his wise and steady guidance. His heart rate never exceeded sixty-seven and his O_2 never dropped below eighty, but I bet he would struggle running twelve miles in 106 degrees in Dallas! The topography was hostile, as was our unstable trail—a mixture of gravel, rocks, and sand. Armed with just water, we left our packs under a rock for the home stretch.

"Just quit! You made it far enough!" the voices in my head urged while *"Henda, la cima es muy cerca, solamente sesenta minutos mas!"* the encouraging voice of my Peruvian mountain guide pressed me to continue. Success can be so close yet so far away. Climbing El Misti volcano to its peak was so much harder than I ever thought it would be.

The last sixty minutes before I reached the summit were excruciatingly difficult. I could see the top just above, but instead of a straight vertical ascent we had to crisscross the steep mountain face in a ceaseless array of switchbacks. The Himalayan 100 race had taught me how much I hated switchbacks, and El Misti volcano confirmed that they could bring me to my knees every time. Exhausted, the ice-cold wind gnawing at me, and with 73% oxygen saturation, my lungs were starved for air. I inched forward and upward, counting thirty steps at a time before allowing myself thirty breaths of rest, hunched over my trekking poles and so grateful for their support. Tunnel vision was all I could pull out of my reserves—just focus on the next thirty steps . . . thirty steps forward, thirty breaths of rest . . .

I had to be reminded why I needed to reach the summit. My reasons all became so unimportant when it was just vital not to quit, to just finish the task, one small step at a time. Suddenly the emergency room in Arequipa became a small dot on the arid terrain of rocks and volcanic sand that surrounded me.

Minutes later I stood at the top, or more accurately, sobbing on my knees in volcanic scree. But as my tears dripped into the volcanic sand and Arequipa lay at my feet very far below, I raised my poles in victory, having finally felt the shadows around me scatter. Liberated from the massive trepidation of dying that I had carried since 2009, I could enjoy the spectacular views. I filed El Misti under "very special" to take out and dust off whenever a kick to the head to count my blessings was in order. The next time I found myself in Arequipa, I would consider climbing Chachani, the adjacent volcano at 20,000 feet. I would just have to bring an ice axe and crampons . . . and far thicker gloves!

One Wheel Down and the Axle Dragging

THE BOEING 767 CABIN was dimly lit and silent as most of my fellow passengers were fast asleep. It was the summer of 2011, and my family and I were more than halfway into our six-hour flight from Anchorage back to Dallas after a vacation. We had spent the past two weeks in an RV touring the rugged land of the north. It was my second excursion to the wild and wonderful that defines Alaska in summer. I'd carried a fantasy about the quintessential American family vacation in an RV, as it didn't get any more white-picket fence than that in my mind! I rented the six-person deluxe model with a master bedroom, another queen bed above the driver's section, and living and dining room seats that collapsed into a double bed. Included were a small kitchen and bathroom. Snug would be a good word to describe it. Compact would also do it justice. Cramped out of my friggin' mind and trapped on wheels would be the honest picture.

When I ask my kids today what they remember most about the family vacation, they recall a similar picture. Apparently I appeared permanently pissed off the entire time. They tiptoed around the RV to not trip my crazy fuse, and generally felt that Mom was a bomb waiting to explode. We arrived in Alaska the first week in June, just days after the 82nd Texas legislature ran its course. I was burned out and mentally exhausted from my time impersonating a lobbyist and politician, especially the last hurried and stress-filled days of the session.

On May 25, five days before the clock ran out, I received a call to come to the capitol as soon as possible to testify in the senate. The senators on the state affairs committee were calling a special hearing immediately following the day's agenda to hear testimony in favor of Henda's Law. HB-834 (the education-only piece) had already died on the vine in the public health committee due to political agendas and special interests. To my surprise, HB-2102 (with the insurance component only) passed in the Texas house and was now on its way to the senate.

But there was a problem. The chances of passing Henda's Law in the senate were slim to none if this bill obligated insurance carriers to pay for the additional screening. In fact the governor threatened to veto the bill as it was. It left us no choice but to switch out the insurance provision with the information and education pieces from the defunct HB-834. Backroom politics, anyone?

We were running out of time to get anything signed at all. By then I felt like an NFL quarterback advancing the ball ten yards at a time with two minutes left in the game and a touchdown short of winning.

Compared to my house testimony, sitting around a very large table on the senate floor while being grilled by senators was up there with cleaning the outside windows of a skyscraper. It was completely terrifying, and great was my joy when it passed unanimously! However, the celebration was very short lived because the bill still had to go back to the house to be reconciled and revoted on the house floor as we had switched the verbiage.

By then it was May 29, with one day left to get Henda's Law signed by both the house and senate before time was up. The final tally of the house vote was Yes 136, No 5, Not Voting 2. As the last grains of sand fell through the top bubble of the hourglass, they sent the signed bill to the governor for his signature on May 30, 2011. It was the 140th day and just hours before it was too late. In hindsight I should have sought out a beach chair under a palm tree on a deserted island to regroup instead of ten days in an RV. I had to set up everyone's beds every night, break them down every morning, plot our route, prepare three meals a day, determine our grey water drops, do laundry for four people every other day, clean, and play tour guide and activities director. You probably would have been mad as hell too!

From our starting point in Anchorage we drove north to

Talkeetna, a small Alaskan town in the shadow of Denali. Small, funky, and quaint, it was the launch pad for many adventurers wanting to conquer North America's tallest peak. Adding to my bracelets from everywhere, I picked up my oldest bracelet there. It dates back 50,000 years and I found it in a little shop in Talkeetna. It is solid silver with oval-shaped disks of wooly mammoth ivory tusks. As the tundra has been slowly melting, these tusks are coming to the surface. The locals use it to carve striking objects and jewelry. I fancy wearing this bracelet because it reminds me of the majesty of Alaska. When it encircles my wrist I feel tied to its land and spirit.

From there we carried on to Denali National Park and parked our mobile motel with views of the spectacular Alaska Range. It seemed almost sacrilegious to be in the presence of such grand views that few have the privilege to experience while filled with shadows and despair. Every day I awoke anxiously hoping that Governor Perry would sign the bill that day, and every night I went to sleep in anguish. I was a yo-yo being pulled back and forth, incapable of being present in God's country.

Growing up in South Africa close to nature gave me a tremendous appreciation for the untamed. Residing in the US, I had not found many truly unspoiled places like Alaska. Its grandeur and size overwhelmed me, and I could sense how nature only tolerated the human dwellings that dotted the landscape. It felt as if it stood ready at any time to engulf them. Being surrounded by eagles, bears, whales, and orcas reminded me of the necessity to have nature near me.

After Denali we headed south toward the Kenai Peninsula and my sour mood continued to fester. While watching the bald eagles in their effortless liftoffs and landings, I fantasized about feeding some of the people I'd met at the capitol in small bites to the eagles. I imagined them being airlifted to nests filled with little bald eagle hatchlings. I know—evil thoughts to be having while surrounded by glaciers, thick forests, and snowcapped mountain ranges.

Our next stop was Seward, another coastal community famous for the original mile zero of the Iditarod—The Last Great Race. I promptly added volunteering one day on the Iditarod to my bucket list. And I don't even like dogs! But the dogs running this race are fine athletes inspiring man to take on nature in an epic challenge. Together they cross 1,000 miles of the remotest, roughest, coldest terrain on the planet. Totally badass, if you ask me!

Orcas were joyously frolicking in the icy waters on our way to the Kenai Fjords National Park. While watching them I was having flashbacks of the strain of sitting in the gallery in the Texas house watching the final debate of HB-2102 before the vote. Our RV crisscrossed the great state of Alaska while I remained the dark storm cloud unable to snap out of my fear that I would fail. If the governor did not sign the bill, all the effort would be for nothing.

In Homer we fished for halibut in the ocean and for king salmon on a remote lake in the Alaskan wilderness that was only accessible by private seaplane. Our bush pilot was a rugged native and detoured to fly us over a glacier and across summer plains filled with moose, brown bears, and grizzly bears. We brought back to Dallas more than seventy pounds of halibut and salmon. After six months of "Henda's fish dishes," my kids suggested that we switch back to beef and chicken permanently! By the way, I'm not sure if you noticed the scene names in this section are dedicated to great Texan speak. I myself didn't know expressions like these and stole them off the internet.

At the end of our vacation we boarded our flight back to Dallas to head home on June 17. It was exactly two years from the day I had been lying in the OR waiting for a large chunk of cancer to be removed from my right breast. My phone rang at 4:00 P.M. as I handed my checked bags to the airline attendant. The bill had been signed into law! Certainly far from perfect, Texas women with dense breast tissue would now receive a letter, after having a mammogram, informing them of vital information that could potentially save their lives. Many Austin lobby chefs cooked up the final verbiage. If I wrote the legislation, I would have used simple English words and shorter sentences, and added a few Oxford commas.

2011 marked my conversion in becoming a pragmatist. I stopped condemning myself for not achieving complete perfection. If moving forward required a few steps back, I no longer gave myself ten lashings with a sjambok before bedtime. Giving it my best has become good enough. And then the chips must fall.

HB-2102 took effect on September 1, 2011, and was fully implemented in all mammogram facilities in Texas by January 1, 2012.

Henda's Law

If your mammogram demonstrates that you have dense breast tissue, which could hide abnormalities, and you have other risk factors for breast cancer that have been identified, you might benefit from supplemental screening tests that may be suggested by your ordering physician. Dense breast tissue, in and of itself, is a relatively common condition. Therefore, this information is not provided to cause undue concern, but rather to raise your awareness and to promote discussion with your physician regarding the presence of other risk factors, in addition to dense breast tissue. A report of your mammogram results will be sent to you and your physician. You should contact your physician if you have any questions or concerns regarding this report.

The Morning After

AND HERE I THOUGHT I was a hero! By early fall in 2011 I ran head-on into the Henda-haters. If only the law was simply identified as House Bill 2102. The backlash from the medical community was crushing. Didn't see it coming. I had planned on wearing a pink superhero cape for Halloween.

Radiologists embraced the disclosure, but many primary care physicians, internal medicine docs, and ob-gyns resented it. It forced changes to the status quo. Oh, and what do you know—also changes to the standard of care.

Many physicians didn't understand dense breast tissue either. Furthermore, they objected to the additional disclosure as it demanded more discussion time during a patient's wellness exam. Time that was not billable. And patients would need supplemental screening that might not be covered by the patients' insurance. I understood their pain and frustration and wanted to hire one of those little planes to fly around with a banner: The Governor Planned to Veto the Insurance!

But I had zero sympathy. Zippy zilch. They were not the ones dying. Some of us were. Watch me care about their discomfort. I knew that Henda's Law was imperfect. But I also completely believed that it would kick start meaningful conversations about how to screen for about half of all women with dense breasts.

My feelings were hurt by the backlash, but my skin was thick enough when I read the criticism on social media and the press. For a while I got a regular weekly fax notice from one ob-gyn advising me to stick to selling houses and stop trying to practice medicine. Week after week I slowly fed his message through my shredder. Friends and clients gladly shared their stories, good and bad, about asking their doctors about their breast density after they received the "You have dense breast tissue" letter.

As a breast cancer survivor I can vouch for how scary it is to be screened—before, during, and after. It is alarming to hear that you have dense breast tissue. Trust me. Being told you have a later-stage breast cancer is way scarier. *Girlfriends, you should embrace the knowledge and get to know the best way to care for those lovely boobies!* Regarding all cancers, I have never wavered in my belief that an early diagnosis is what we all deserve. That's where "survival" lives. I don't care who is scared and who is pissed off. My activism emerged from my anger about not having the opportunity to manage my breast care or an early cancer diagnosis. I'm still a little pissed off. And about that insurance veto—I was furious at the stupidity of politics for several years, as me and my gang in Austin tried in vain in 2013 and 2015 to get that portion of the bill passed.

Ta da! Which brings us to the 85th Texas legislature in 2017. Sweet revenge. I was not running the ball this time, and House

Bill 1036 was in expert, professional lobbyist hands. But I was watching the play-by-play back in Dallas. The bill would cover 3D mammography during a woman's wellness exam. What the heck is 3D? Still far from peeing on a stick, it's the latest emerging technology in mammography. Does it catch all? No. Does it catch more tumors and penetrate dense breast tissue better? Yes. Do I sleep a little better at night? Yes. Am I a fan of Texas politics? Hell, no!

In 2011 Texas was just the second state to pass breast density legislation. By the middle of 2017 only ten states in the United States were left without an enacted law, an introduced law, or active legislation of a bill regarding dense breast tissue. We surpassed the tipping point years before. The many grassroots efforts to change how we care for dense breasts are important, as it was (and is) about life and death. And we all choose life. Boobs and all.

Who matters most to me? The women who call and email me to share their stories about their breast cancer, annual screenings, dense breasts, and lumps. And the ones who ask me to help them. Their faith in my guidance through this convoluted nightmare has become my most cherished way of connection. Its power brings me comfort and validates that together we are strong and will survive. I also care about the many hundreds of thousands who think I'm just some breast law without a face and story.

Tell your heart that the fear of suffering is worse than the suffering itself. And that no heart has ever suffered when it goes in search of its dreams, because every second of the search is a second's encounter with God and with eternity.

When a person really desires something, all the universe conspires to help that person to realize his dream.

—THE ALCHEMIST, PAULO COELHO

Solo and Filled with Sorrow

WHAT TO DO WITH my wedding gown? It had been cocooned in a blue plastic garment bag for almost twenty years. It seemed wrong to donate it to Goodwill or toss it in the trash. Never dry cleaned, the ivory silk was slightly yellowed. Some old red wine stains near the hem were the whistleblowers that the dress was worn once in celebration. My daughter's expression confirmed when asked—she certainly didn't want to inherit the burden of wearing it down any aisle.

After brainstorming online, I found the Angel Gown® Program and mailed my dress off to them the next day. It's a national charity whose seamstresses convert donated wedding gowns into delicate baby garments. These little gowns are shipped to NICUs around the country for grieving families and allow them to dress their babies for their burial. Somehow it seemed fitting for my gown to be repurposed to bring comfort and honor to families in their dark hours, to share the loss of what is not to be.

Divorce sucks. In my raw ivory silk dress embroidered with delicate lace, I vowed "until death us do part" on my wedding day. I surely didn't plan to one day stand in front of a judge and recite the no-fault intention to divorce the father of my children.

I can spin all sorts of pretty tales and good-looking words about my "sickness" hand of cards. How my near-death stints woke me up. Blah, blah, blah. I could. But I hope you would call me out! More than halfway into this story we both know that I faked my way into the "wife" role from the start. So then allow me to be candid. Let's cut through the cliché crap. I finally had the courage to acknowledge that my husband and I were (and are) good people but desperately incompatible. I'm jumping ahead. But can you guess the number-one reason why men dumped me while dating post-divorce? I'm "too much." Seriously. What the eff does that even mean? Too much of what? Yeah. Join the dating confusion zombie zone. But that's in the next section. Hang with me while I'm getting divorced first.

We tried hard staying together while making a living and raising kids. We wanted each other to blend into the roles we had created for the other while dating. I cannot speak for him, but I certainly had no foggy idea what I wanted beyond my initial ticket to the "family" party. Our early years were good but the first real fractures showed after Nicky's memorial and my return from South Africa.

You can imagine being married one minute to uncomplicated and then suddenly your spouse begins to float the idea of moving to

South Africa and taking the kids "road schooling" across the world for a few years. Freaky, if you weren't an enthusiast of the Texas Giant roller coaster at the local Six Flags amusement park. The next few pages are important to me. My editor encouraged me to cut it short, but I ignored her advice. I want you to come with me on the journey that led to my separation in the spring of 2012. Indulge me. I need you to step through this debris with me. Let's spend Thanksgiving 2011 together in Prague after Henda's Law passed. I was a raging lunatic wreck in a very unpretty way.

Prague? Why Prague? Really? In the winter? Yes, and in the absence of eating turkey and celebrating Thanksgiving. I could argue that I went by myself because I wanted to step away and spend time alone. Bottom line? Neither of us chose to have Thanksgiving together as a family. He and our kids went to visit his family and I opted last minute for the Golden City, the Paris of the East, in lieu of drowning in misery at our home in Dallas. Although I traveled often, it had been twenty-two years since I was all alone for ten days in a foreign place.

I discovered that all our large luggage pieces had busted zippers forty-five minutes before I had to leave for the airport. After running to a store nearby I had fifteen minutes left to pack for a ten-day trip in the middle of the winter. My bag was a disaster. In every way. Dragging that bag through the airports, train stations, and bus stations in Europe was a sick joke I played on myself. And reflective of the convoluted state I found myself in.

The bus to Prague arrived from Germany, where my plane had landed just as the early dark of a winter's night settled over the city. I caught glimpses from the bus window of the impressive buildings lining the river whose name was still unfamiliar. My small hotel, dating back to the fifteenth century, was in the Old City near the castle and the Charles Bridge on Nerudova Street.

I had resisted purchasing a guidebook, opting to discover Prague without any preconceived suggestions and interpretations. Armed with only the pocket-sized map from the hotel receptionist, I headed south toward what I now identified as the Vltava River. Night was in full swing when I turned the corner and feasted my hungry eyes on the Charles Bridge. I wanted to send a personalized note to the city of Prague staffer in charge of spotlighting buildings and statues: "Dear Sir/Madam, you stopped me in my tracks, left me speechless and briefly gasping for air. I sincerely appreciate the splendid view you presented to a forlorn tracker searching for happiness and who she is. Regards, Henda."

Prague showed me much loveliness in the days following. However, if I were to choose only one word to describe its charm, it would be "music." In the city of Dvorak and Mozart, music burst from its seams and enfolded me tenderly in the brilliant notes of the great maestros. It flowed like the Vltava River from the buildings to the street performers and through the many people walking with a violin or cello case strapped to their backs.

Opera in Prague is like eating a gyro from the street vendor guy at the corner of 46th and Broadway in NYC. Utterly divine and the best gyros in North America! My chance to see Don Giovanni in the Estates Theatre where Mozart debut it first in 1787 was unreal. I had a box seat and felt briefly like I belonged to the European uppity-up. Singlehandedly my finest opera moment ever.

Along with my favorite routes in the Old City, I also quickly designated my preferred street performers and strolled by their specific spots on my daily walks. Among them there was Alex . . . always on the Charles Bridge at night. He played the Bohemian crystal water glasses. Its haunting sound tapped into a "Henda" frequency foreign to me. Alex excelled at making my tears flow freely every night while I listened to his water melodies in the subzero air while hugging myself.

It was during those nights when the debate whether to stay in an unfulfilling marriage for my kids' sake or to give it up early raged inside my head and heart without a winner either way. On one side I wanted to stick it out until both kids had graduated from high school, but the depth of my unhappiness was not a place where I wanted to linger. The memory from early 2009 was still fresh about how dark my night could be. I was averse to reenacting the libretto where I get hopelessly lost. Prague bore witness to how worthless, unwanted, and unloved I felt. I found myself stranded in the confinement of my own mind, unable to escape. Like my right breast's scar, I felt damaged. At forty-five years old I had a ninety-year-old blemished soul.

Real estate was my distraction. I focused on my clients' needs to navigate their transitions while ignoring my own. Between work, various breast cancer volunteer activities, and training for my next endurance race, I numbed myself from my glaring inadequacy at being happily married.

The whipping pain of keeping up the appearance of bliss left unfathomable welts inside me. I was a fraud, not just to my friends and myself, but mostly to my two budding teenagers. What was I teaching them about honesty, love, and happiness? What example was I setting to live a half-assed existence instead of one filled with joy? How could I be their mother and not give them my best version? Was I willing to sacrifice all just so I could claim the prize of "still married"? What a coward I was! God showed me how fragile my breath was. Did I not learn those lessons enough?

Alex's music set the stage to my Prague ritual as it unfolded nightly after dinner. I would make my way up Nerudova Street past my hotel to the castle and the cathedral, which was also one of the highest points in the city. I would sit quietly on their stone walls, contemplating the view in front of me, with just the moon, stars, and streetlights as companions, and I would eavesdrop on myself. One of the unintended consequences of solo travel is a vow of silence. Inadvertently your conversations are limited to the brief interaction with waiters, street vendors, and hotel staff. Now add to this quiet cocktail a country whose language is completely foreign and you don't only hear the voices in your own head but you start to converse with them.

I observed my Thanksgiving within the austere walls of St. George's Basilica near the Castle. For more than a thousand years it had stood witness to people seeking solace within. How fortunate I was to stumble upon a music concert of Vivaldi, Mozart, Bizet, Handel, and Brahms on a day of giving thanks. Exiting the basilica, night had fallen. Inspired by my surroundings and the music, I entered a small antique shop I'd seen earlier.

Inside I found an exquisite bracelet, circa the early 1920s. It was solid silver with several intricate filigreed Egyptian scenes encircling its delicate frame, including the Great Sphinx of Giza, the three pyramids, and a scarab beetle. Feeling our joint displacement, I wondered how we had ended up in a Prague store. Wearing it while I wandered the streets also connected me to the women whose wrists it had encircled for the past century. I suspected that we could share many stories of a kindred journey of lonely despair. In the months following, the Sphinx became my benevolent guardian and the scarab my own amulet of a future rebirth and renewal.

Without a Fight

MERCIFULLY, REASON INTERVENED IN early 2012 when my husband and I jointly decided it best to part ways. Would my marriage have survived had I not brushed intimately against death? I don't know. Maybe and maybe not. The reality is it didn't. Regardless, I'm proud how we dissolved and managed unraveling our complex tapestry spanning more than twenty years. Our children are our forever bond. It was in the separating when we proved the strength of our commitment to do what was right and fair for them and each other. Above our differences, we put the interest of our children as our priority and allowed the rest to gradually fade.

It was in their best interest for us to gently and slowly navigate the stormy waters of separation. We decided to keep them in their childhood home and instead we would be the ones to switch back and forth. I put my real estate expertise to good use and found for us a one-bedroom condo nearby. Their dad and I switched every two days and alternated weekends between our home and the condo. We shared the same bedroom but not simultaneously. We put no deadline on the transition and instead allowed time to be our guide about what was best for us as a family.

Two years would pass before "divorce" became the new checkbox on our application forms. I lived out of a suitcase for most of the time while my shoes dwelled in the trunk of my car. Some days I would arrive on our street about to turn into the driveway when I realized that I was supposed to sleep at the condo instead. The unspoken rule was that you left the condo in the same condition you found it—tidy and neat—dishes done, bed made, and your stuff picked up or taken with you.

Our kids thrived and their lives for the most part were uninterrupted. Their friends still came for parties and sleepovers. As their mom and dad, we were present together at all school and sporting events and parent meetings. We made it clear to all our friends and family that there was no war and no sides to be picked. I still attended many Salmeron family gatherings, and we slowly learned how to get divorced while staying together. The lessons were good and the outcome one of my proudest accomplishments. The two of us found a better way of dividing our lives than to rip its fabric in two.

Instead of opting to use attorneys to distribute our assets and stir the pot to keep the billable hours coming their way, we used an Excel spreadsheet at the kitchen table. I bought the paralegal software to draft our parenting plan as we, after all, knew what was best for us. We hired an attorney to file our paperwork and the final tally in legal fees was "bare bones" for Dallas County. I no longer think of my marriage as a failure. Instead I received the two most prized gifts imaginable— my cherished children. Although no longer a full-time member, I'm extremely grateful that I'm still part of an extended family spanning three continents who never closed their doors or hearts on me.

The Crash of 2012

FIVE WEEKS. THAT'S HOW many days it took before I could wash the Kalahari Desert sand out. For five weeks, my gear bag and I had a silent stare off each time I entered my bathroom. "Unpack me." "No, I'm not ready, bugger off!" "Unpack me . . . ignoring me won't make me go away!" "I'm not ready!" Inside the bag hid the memories I was not yet prepared for. I didn't want to look at the T-shirt that I didn't earn the right to wear. I didn't want to put away my bib number and checkpoint card with all the unmarked time slots.

The "Big Daddy" of South Africa, the Kalahari Augrabies Extreme, is a 150-mile ultra-endurance race over seven days and six stages, fully self-supported. To quote: *Participants must carry all their supplies, clothes and compulsory safety/survival equipment for the duration of the event. Overnight shelter in camps, and water, which is strictly controlled and distributed during the race, is supplied. The event goes way beyond merely covering 150 miles in extreme conditions; it is a challenge to get past what normal people would regard as crazy, and achieve one's personal goals.*

Squeezing all my food, clothes, medical kit, sleeping bag, and pad into a running backpack required great compromise. Particularly as it bumped into my "Just in Case" style to travel with a small convenience store. I spent months researching gear and taste-tested my way through all the freeze-dried meals from my local REI store. My final pack weighed twenty-six pounds without the mandatory 1.5 liters of water we had to carry.

I wanted this race to rescue me from the angst of my looming separation from my husband. I so desperately craved to feel the adrenaline rush of a finish line, a medal, and a T-shirt. In those moments I felt so alive and unstoppable, on top of my world, where I could reach out and effortlessly touch each star within my dreams. The validation of accomplishment collided against my acute despair of failure. I wanted to walk away a winner and bask in the warmth of victory. Even if it was the short-lived high of an endurance race.

Instead, still trapped inside my race pack, my sweat could tell you about the day in the Kalahari when I dropped out of the race. I instantly changed from an endurance runner to a volunteer. For the next four days I was assigned to a checkpoint handing out water and giving comfort to my race buddies. Helping them to reach the finish afforded me an intimate view into what it took to complete a fully self-supported race. I should have tattooed "Rookie" and "Clueless" on my forehead.

I was a volunteer at the last checkpoint on the long stage on Day Five and most runners reached us between 3:00–5:00 A.M. after unending hours on their feet. Their eyes had the vacant look of unspeakable mental and physical exhaustion and confirmed that it would take a lot for me to accomplish my own ambition to finish a race such as this. My experience from the sidelines taught me much more about race preparation, nutrition, hydration, and pain and blister management than being a novice endurance runner ever could.

I often revisited 1:25 P.M. on Day Two, when I decided to withdraw from the race. Such a nice word, withdraw. So much kinder than loser, quitter, flop . . . sigh. I know. Please. I had heard it all.

Showing up at the start already made me a winner. Only forty-five people out of more than 7.3 billion signed up. I didn't quit, I was injured. Yeah. But that didn't make it any easier accepting my first DNF—did not finish. It was also painful to honestly confess that I wasn't properly prepared. Period. No excuses. No BS. I was not. And it was clear long before 1:25 P.M. on Day Two, when it was 122°F under a thorn tree in the Kalahari Desert . . . when I quit.

I doubted myself the weeks leading up to the race when I hurt a tendon in my foot. I missed a step while buying ice cream with my daughter. I questioned myself even more on the bus ride to the Kalahari when one of my new race friends commented that my race pack was too heavy compared to my body weight. And self-doubt raged inside me when I stumbled on my first sandy riverbeds on Day One. I had never walked in sand like that, let alone run! Regardless of the heat, my chances of finishing slowly dimmed.

Self-supported races change the playing field for wannabe runners like me. When you have to strap on a pack in the desert and carry all your supplies for seven days, you have just entered the endurance race version of the Hunger Games. You can be taken out by so many variables and your margin for error shrinks from small, to very slim, and then to none. Like before, being mentally tough, I thought I was capable to reach the finish line.

On all these types of races there is a sweeper behind the last runner. They remove the course markings and make sure that no runner is left behind. Could I just say one thing? I never want to be swept again. Ever. It screwed with my headspace. I knew he was waiting for me. Sitting under a tree watching me struggle through the perpetual sand. I would listen to his quad bike engine, needing him to speed up to come say hi, simultaneously wanting him to go away and let me fight through my torment. He became my insurance policy on Day Two when I limped from tree to tree. When I sought validation at 1:25 P.M. on Day Two that it was perhaps not a good idea to continue. After consulting with the race doctor, we concurred that my patella tendon was sprained from a steep climb out of a gorge earlier that day, and continuing might cause a more serious long-term injury. I was taken to the crew camp with several other racers who were the other casualties of Day Two from a combination of injuries, dehydration, and illness.

I struggled with my decision and second-guessed myself over and over. What if I just went to the next checkpoint? What if, what if, what if... Ugh! I met a seasoned racer recently who gave me sound advice: Never doubt your judgment from battle. Trust your gut's voice then. Looking back the picture always looks different. Okay. Fine. I did the right thing. I withdrew because it was the smart choice under that thorn tree on that day when it was so hot. When I limped with 125 miles and five days left. I made a rookie mistake and had a pack that was ten pounds too heavy. I had to learn to shed holding on to "Just in Case" if I wanted to participate in self-supported endurance races!

After returning to Dallas I probed my racing motives for five weeks while fighting with my gear bag. What did I want to achieve with ultra-endurance racing? Was it just about a T-shirt and medal? To just finish? A race notch on my headboard? Proving to myself that I had survived cancer and a heart attack because I feared my own death? NO! I enjoyed how ultra-endurance races pushed me beyond my limits. I depended on the exercise regularly to be reminded that

I could go past what might seem insane to most people. I just didn't get challenged enough day to day. I wanted to take myself to a place where I could find my sense of self over and over. Where I could come face to face with the force inside me that guided me always to keep moving forward. I needed the affirmation that it was intact and solid. I found comfort in that I had a strain of toughness in me to endure and go beyond. I loved feeling freedom from ordinary, from normal, from being part of the herd. On a race I basked in the shared struggle with my fellow runners and friends to overcome hardship and find our strength together.

Failure never tasted good. My marriage had ended in separation just before I left for the Kalahari race. The Kalahari Desert was wise not to offer me its raft when I was not ready to reach the shore on my own. I washed my gear bag and its sweaty contents on December 1, 2012, when my training kicked off for the next self-supported race I registered for: The Grand to Grand Ultra scheduled for September 2013. The north rim of the Grand Canyon and I had a date then—it was the next wonder on my path and I planned to dress up for the occasion.

I was ready to shed my "Just in Case" mindset and commit to what is required for me to reach the finish line of a fully self-supported ultra-extreme endurance race: grit, perseverance, and the willingness to bear tremendous pain and discomfort. Yeah. Story of my life. This is my sport. We understand each other. I'm all in.

Under a Desert Sky

SEVEN A.M. I HAD been cocooned in my sleeping bag for less than two hours, fully clothed and exhausted beyond logic. My feet were a throbbing and swollen mess covered in blisters and a chilling reality that I could drop out of the race at any checkpoint. It was the start of Day Four on the long stage of Grand to Grand, a six-stage and seven-day fully self-supported footrace spanning 170 miles from the north rim of the Grand Canyon to the summit of the Pink Cliffs of the Grand Staircase in Utah.

I had already covered ninety-six miles over three days and had just spent twenty-four hours on my feet in the effort to complete the fifty-four miles of this stage. I arrived at Checkpoint Six at 4:30 A.M. after a grueling eight miles over four hours in the dark of night. Never had I been enveloped in total darkness and had to navigate my way by the small beam of my headlamp. The dim trail marked by LED lights scattered across the black of night was fraught with steep, sandy, and unsteady terrain. "Keep moving" was the constant mantra of my meditation as I compelled my legs and feet to execute the demands of my mind. My fifteen-pound race pack was digging hard into my shoulders and back and the craving to drop it became overwhelming.

Checkpoint Six had hot water and was one of the sleeping checkpoints on the 54-mile stage. Mercilessly, the desert had lessons to teach me and had commenced the class at Checkpoint Four. I met a fellow runner, as he was also one of the last two racers making the cutoff. He was in bad shape and wanted to quit. *Quit. Really? No way! No bloody way!* I convinced him to continue to Checkpoint Five, six miles ahead of us. Saving him from giving up became my focus. Although I felt strong and able to run, I matched his speed of less than 1.5 miles an hour, thereby adding significant time to my own race clock. He stayed behind at Checkpoint Five.

Lesson 187: withdrawing from a race is a very personal decision. Lesson 261: slogging through the desert in the pitch black of night in your own company sucks. Lesson 354: feeling sorry for yourself is your problem. Lesson 900: giving in and giving up are separated by one vowel. One lets you surrender and the other lets you stop. The desert has taught me that when I just yield, I can go farther.

Dawn broke as I left Checkpoint Six with approximately seventeen miles left after a short reprieve and a much-needed cup of hot soup. The next four miles spanned the Coral Pink Sand Dunes in Utah. Near Zion National Park, this is the only major sand dune field on the Colorado Plateau. I timed my departure so that I would see the sunrise across the dunes. I expected that crossing the dunes after having already been on my feet for twenty-four hours would be tough, I just didn't know how challenging.

I was the last runner to leave the checkpoint and chilly shadows of early morning covered the sand dunes. Daunted, and with the wind whipping hard at my body, I sought out my mantra of "keep moving" to focus my mind on the task at hand. Each step made me sink calf-length into the sand. My gaiters kept the soft pink grains from eroding my blistered feet any further but the exhausted effort to dig my legs out of the abyss with each step was staggering.

So often I have run into pure magic. Sometimes it has been while scuba diving, or on mountaintops, or in the simple pleasure of a spectacular sunset under a big sky in Dallas. Frequently it was because I intentionally sought out the magic in the art of living a life lived well. As I stood on the edge of the north rim at the start of this immense personal challenge on Day One, I wished that my gorges and canyons could be so breathtaking if I allowed my rivers to run unhindered through my consciousness. While admiring the vastness that nature presented me with, I desired for my soul to embrace the limitless miracle of my own humanity. Standing on its edge surrounded by the many hues of the prehistoric rock formations carved by the Colorado River over millions of years, I could just bow my head and offer my gratitude to be in its presence.

The Alchemist by Paulo Coelho was on my ninth-grader's summer reading list and out of boredom on a flight from Costa Rica I read it. What a read. What a story. If you had not yet read it, read it now. As I watched the sun that morning in Utah over those dunes, stripped of every ounce of veneer, exhausted and on my knees in the sand, I discovered I too was an alchemist.

(Alchemy is the art of liberating parts of the cosmos from temporal existence and achieving perfection that for metals is gold, and for man longevity, then immortality, and finally redemption. Thanks, Wikipedia.)

Santiago sets out to find his destiny and personal legend. After an extended journey he had to transform himself into the wind to save himself from execution. As the wind whipped around me and sand hurled itself against my skin on the dunes, I realized I could become the wind. Like Santiago I believe that when we reach through the soul of the world and see it is part of the soul of God, we discover it is also our own soul. And we can perform small miracles every day.

I finished the 54-mile long stage in thirty-one hours. It was brutal, unforgiving, and liberating. It pushed me to beyond what I thought possible and sliced a gorgeous slot canyon through my being. I went on to finish the 170 miles of the Grand to Grand ultra-extreme race and earned my finisher belt buckle and T-shirt. Many moments during the seven days left me breathless and inspired by the loveliness of nature and the triumph of the human spirit to prevail. However, sunrise across the sand dunes in Utah is forever stamped on my heart. Unforgettable and utterly grand.

And did you get what you wanted from this life, even so?
I did.
And what did you want?
To call myself beloved, to feel myself beloved on the earth.

—"LATE FRAGMENT," RAYMOND CARVER

Love Unleashed

MY WRITING GREW FROM a desperate place where I was afraid that my children wouldn't know their mother. If I died I was terrified that the only point of reference for them as the years passed would be vague vignettes of a woman holding them and giving them soft kisses. They were only eight and ten when my longevity was questionable. Think back. At that age we don't really remember much detail. I love them more than any other love I have ever known. Not only would I die for them, I would kill anyone who would hurt them callously. Like the Creep.

I had the bursting need of immortality to tell them my story, to voice my dreams, beliefs, and fears, and to ensure that they knew me. There was only one way to guarantee the accuracy and it was to tell them the narrative of my life in writing. In my own words. My early attempts were the stunted efforts of a foreigner trying to express myself in a language I could speak, read, and write. But I could not write the authentic words that were trapped inside me. So much for my outward pretense of being "English." The keys to unlocking the message from my heart and soul in writing were as elusive as to grasp the winter fog of an early dawn across the meadow. Visible, but entirely out of my reach.

But the intense desire to leave my children with the knowledge of who their mother was became far stronger than my insecurity of baring myself in English. Months of struggle dissolved into moments of fluency. I was proud of the collection of words that formed sentences to become paragraphs. Together, they became pages. Each one to articulate my sincere conversation about my life's journey. My gift to my children. And more so, to allow me to rummage through my own junk and separate the keepers from what needed to be discarded. I had to become brave enough to share my heart with you, my dark and ugly parts side by side with my light. I had to brace myself to be willing to be judged. This book is not a novel. It is my life story. I'm giving you the power to take it apart page by page and shoot your arrows. Go ahead. My shields are down and I don't mind your scrutiny.

The words that emerged slowly chipped away at the armor I had clad myself in for most of my life, to reveal to me the person I could and wanted to become. I felt a close kinship with a true master of his craft. If I was on the Little League baseball bench, he was MVP of the World Series. But in a very small way, I related. His *David* lives at the Accademia Gallery in Florence and we visited him during our family summer trip in 2016. When I had last seen *David* in 1988 while backpacking through Europe, he was covered in scaffolding and being restored.

My kids were more interested in the nearby gelato cafes than admiring a Renaissance nude male masterpiece by Michelangelo. But a deal was a deal. Visiting one marble statue in exchange for the melting deliciousness of Italian ice cream on your tongue. After dragging them to all the art museums in Paris, their enthusiasm for the Florence treasures was low.

Ten years earlier I had promised my daughter and her cousin that I would take them to Paris and Italy for their sixteenth birthday. She gently reminded me a few months before their birthdays about my pledge. Luckily I found cheap airfare and my son did not object when I brought him with us.

Inside the museum, we progressed down the main hall toward the center where *David* was holding court under a halolike dome. It was packed and I had my usual freak-out with very large crowds. That was when I found them. The *Prisoners* or *Slaves*. The four larger-than-life unfinished marble sculptures by Michelangelo. I felt that he carved them for me to be found 500 years later. Like a message in a bottle. He was the master to release them from their marble confines. From the *Awakening Slave* to *Atlas,* Michelangelo freed them one at a time. Each is incomplete and the marble shows the chipping scars from its creator. His chisel did not try to be perfect; instead it allowed each image to share their evolution with us. I would never dream to compare myself to him. But I know that if we met at a little Italian café we would have had much to talk about. He was the master, but as a student, I would have absorbed his every word. Particularly the part about letting our imperfections show.

Regardless of my insecure fears, these pages are my unfinished work of my own slaves. I now know that "Mother" is an honor earned and just giving birth to a child does not automatically entitle you to claim the label. Far from trying to hold myself out as perfect, my kids' unconditional love filled the cracks of my own fractured parts with gold. Instead of hiding my damage, like the fine art of Japanese kintsugi, our bond mended me and allowed me to have the courage to display a richer me. The knowing ties of profound loss had gently woven its sturdy threads around our hearts. I almost lost my life and they nearly lost their mother at a young age. Our together times came without the usual burden of the growing pains typical of the teenage years.

We celebrated my first anniversary post my breast cancer diagnosis together in South Africa during the summer of 2010. Taking my kids to Makwassie was an important stop. Not only to show them the refuge from my childhood, but also to feast on Tienie's delicious food and hear stories from when I was a young girl. My mother was raised on a farm nearby but not much was known about her upbringing. She left home as a sixteen-year-old high school dropout to get married, which left her estranged from her father. My grandmother died from cancer when my mother was twelve years old and my grandfather remarried shortly after. It was the 1950s in rural South Africa and no farmer was going to take on the task of raising a teenage girl.

Regrettably, I never met my grandfather and nobody knows when he died. He was known throughout the region to lend money to help farmers acquire their own land. In modern terms, he was a second-lien lender and would loan the difference between what the person could afford and what they could borrow from the bank. Additionally, my grandfather owned large parcels of land and did land appraisals for the banks in the area. Being a residential real estate broker today, I do feel a strange connection to him. He was respected and known as kind, trying to help people. I like to think he was a good and honorable man. I feel cheated that I didn't know him.

One night, under a cloudless star-strewn Makwassie sky I knew so well, I told William about the "Kitty" confession about Gert. His response was unexpected. What about DNA testing? William was agreeable to sibling testing and for $179 I could remove all doubt about my origins. That's very cheap, compared to a lifetime of searching for the truth. A simple cotton swab from our cheeks could determine my belonging. One molecule of life could tell me what I searched for for most of mine. I left the farm unable to decide if that was what I wanted.

Our next stop was Victoria Falls—another wonder of the natural world and one of my seven. Locally called Mosi-oa-Tunya, the Smoke that Thunders, it is located between Zimbabwe and Zambia. It's the largest curtain of falling water. Immense in scope, no picture or words can capture the sound of its roar, the rainbows in its midst, or the inverted rain of the spray that shoots upward from the edge. As I stood encircled within my kids' hugs surrounded by this phenomenon, these God moments, strung together, had created my own intimate prayer beads. I was so grateful for the second chance that life awarded me to choose another way beyond deception, hate, and unhappiness to celebrate my African within. I happily slurp every morsel from the marrowbones of each day.

The trip was crowned by an elephant-back safari nearby and

although maybe tourist cheesy to some, riding on Jake was a blast! His regal gait through the bush while rhythmically flapping his massive ears allowed me a vantage point unlike any I had ever experienced. Afterward, while feeding him his post-ride snack, I gazed into his intelligent eyes, counting his eyelashes, and was curious whether he and the whale shark in Belize the year earlier were related.

Dining at Nature's Enchanted Buffet

THE FIRST CHRISTMAS POST-DIVORCE with my kids, I chose not to try to replicate the Salmeron family traditions of their childhood. Instead I decided that my mark on my kids would continue to be exploring the earth and tasting its bounty of adventure and fun. Already well traveled since toddlers, I wanted to instill in them a lifelong passion for discovering the cathedrals not built by man and the treasures not measured in any currency.

I purposefully picked the far Northwest Territories of Canada as our destination for the holidays to find the elusive Northern Lights as it had been on my bucket list for a while. Once perceived as omens and prophecies, their radiance promised to stir my essence as I witnessed nature's most impressive light show personally. Mysterious and as natural as air, finding them takes special effort if you don't live in the far north. We arrived on Christmas Eve 2013 in Yellowknife, just 250 miles south of the Arctic Circle, and it was -35°F. Frigid, icy, freezing, frosty . . . sorry, none of these words accurately describe what "cold" feels like! My eyelashes were frozen after a short walk down the block and little icicles quickly formed around the hairs in my nose.

I rented arctic gear for us as the warmth of our own Colorado ski clothes was utterly inadequate. Even then you find yourself dressed in four layers more under the bulk of your outerwear. After an hour outside on a snowmobile, I had to bite back the tears as my feet and hands were hurting so much from the cold. Yellowknife sits on the north shore of the Great Slave Lake, the deepest lake in North America at 2,014 feet, and the tenth largest in the world. And it was cold beyond your wildest imagination . . . oh wait . . . I said that already. How about bitter cold? When a portion of an enormous lake becomes an annual ice road about eight inches thick, try bloody hell cold!

Daylight was short each day and the sun never traveled much higher than barely across the horizon. Despite the hostile conditions we learned to ice fish—what an insane lesson in patience while freezing your ninnies off! We huddled together in what can only be described as a small six-seater fish house on skis and tracks—think enclosed snowmobile with bar stools and no amenities. After we learned how to use an auger (okay, I looked up what the thing was called!) and drilled our holes, our "house" backed up over them. For the next two hours we waited for some stupid fish to swim by while we had to keep scooping out ice to prevent the holes from freezing. Our guide had a state-of-the-art GPS system and we did see one fish within view of the little camera. I had never thought the day would come when I would talk to a fish but I almost begged him to come die. Please don't think because the fishing shelter had "house" in its name that it implied warmth or comfort. Respect to all the ice fishermen—you have courage and ice you-know-what!

No Arctic adventure would be complete without learning to

mush and dog sled. Even as a non-dog aficionado, I could get into the sport if it was run anywhere but in snow and ice. It practically made our ice-fishing expedition appear tropical. I had never been so cold standing behind a pack of dogs on a sled. I lost all feeling in my hands and feet and the only reason I didn't cry was because I worried my tears would freeze my eyeballs off and leave me blind. Regarding being a volunteer on the Iditarod dog-sled race? Scratch it.

At 9:00 p.m. on Christmas Eve we drove thirty minutes out onto the Great Slave Lake on snowmobiles to a little cabin away from Yellowknife's lights. Our guide explained that optimum aurora viewings necessitated clear and cold nights (check!) and usually occurred between 10:00 p.m. to 4:00 a.m. Without any guarantee that there would be any aurora, my expectations were childishly high that my Christmas dream would come true. After about an hour, hazy green ribbons began crossing the sky. Elated, I rapidly took pictures, hoping to capture their beauty. Slowly they intensified and my camera could display reds surrounding the green invisible to the naked eye. The butt-freezing Arctic air caused us to linger for just brief intervals before we had to seek warmth inside the cabin.

Ten minutes past midnight on Christmas morning, the sky burst open with a light show my imagination could have never envisioned. The solar wind collided with Earth's magnetic field at that moment and produced a magnificent array of colors. Red, green, violet, and orange ribbons twirled and skipped above the frozen tundra. Covering the entire night sky and dwarfing the stars, it was as if the glory of God danced across the heavens. I wanted to reach up and snuggle within its visual overload. But like all the other wonders I encountered, all I could do was allow myself to be swept into a sensory celebration of life. I was grateful that my camera had run out of battery power earlier, because no picture could ever capture these images. On the snowmobile back to town, while still surrounded by their majesty, my entire being felt enveloped in love and gratitude and I didn't notice how cold it was.

Costa Rica Heartbreak Hotel

THE RAIN PELTED DOWN against my tent and sounded like an angry animal looking for food. I was very proud I could pitch it in the dark by the weak light of my headlamp. The rain flap kept me perfectly dry but even while the rain poured mercilessly down, the heat was sweltering inside my tent. Stripped down to the bare necessities, little rivers of sweat still formed in the many crevices of my skin and ran down to form small puddles next to my deflated sleeping pad. God, it was humid. I was so hot and so dreadfully tired. My feet were trashed—raw, bleeding, and throbbing to the touch. On the other hand my foot bones felt as if they had been slowly crushed between two heavy-duty clamps. The effort to walk back from the dining tent to my simple shelter for the night was almost unbearable.

Our camp was in the jungle and although next to a beach, there was no reprieve from the oppressive jungle heat. My Garmin told me that it was 2:00 A.M. I had been awake for hours, unable to sleep as my sleeping pad had sprung a leak earlier. As the novice camper I was, I hadn't picked my tent site well and was paying the price. I missed the part that one should remove the rocks and stones from underneath your tent as you would be sleeping on said pointy and very sharp objects. Without a working pad, I was in for many hours of misery. The rocks dug into every inch of my aching body and I futilely tried to mold my form around their unyielding and hostile shapes.

My sorrow matched my physical discomfort. In the dark my tears and sweat fused and together with my sobs became the savage creature inside my tent crying out. After dating for almost two years on and off, I had purposefully broken up with him on the way to the airport just days earlier. The jungle was the perfect place to torch my wishful thinking for a "forever" fantasy that I'd made up entirely in my own head. I anticipated that the forceful self-inflicted race pain could cleanse my heart's agony in some small measure.

Initially I'd thought I met my prince. The first spring I wrote his name in the wet sand on a boundless, windswept beach and circled it with a seashell-decorated heart. Our months were filled with warmth, laughter, and joy. He called me "Boer Girl" and I fit perfectly into the curve of his arm next to his heartbeat against my ear. Texan to his center, our differences were legendary and few of our likes were matched. If we followed the rules of compatibility, we should not have made it past a first date. Naively, I planned our future together and I wanted it to last like fine leather that becomes soft and supple over time.

After my first day of the 2015 Coastal Challenge in Costa Rica, my blistered feet could attest that Costa Rica was not for the lightweight, the wannabe, and the unprepared. I switched on Day Two to the shorter distance but still struggled to make it to the end. I found myself often collapsed on the dense jungle floor praying that a deadly snake or spider would rescue me from the misery of having to get up and keep moving. My collection of blisters grew and my respect for my environment increased tenfold. Most of the damage to my feet occurred on Day Two when we crossed several jungle streams and river estuaries while my feet remained wet and muddy for far too long.

My secluded hours in the jungle allowed for much reflection. We had started dating while we both were separated. Our attachment grew from the pain and disappointment of our failed marriages. Like life rafts we held on to each other. I could see our love story being made into a summer blockbuster if only I had tried a little harder to make it last. My obsession to fix our damaged links blinded me from the honest reality that I would suffocate in his world and he would acutely resent mine. Despite my aspirations, our life's rhythms were not in sync. The insecurity of my own worthiness also made me doubt that I was good enough to be his chosen and beloved.

Day Three opened with an eight-mile stretch down an isolated beach, Playa Ballena. With no shade in sight the sun was as much a predator seeking my weak spot as the rain and rocks just hours later in the friendless confinement of my tent. Until I could add speed to my racing, I often found myself alone on the trail. Playa Ballena was not just an area where the humpback whales came during the winter, but the beach formed an actual gigantic whale's tail visible from the air. It witnessed my physical struggle and watched the tormented battle I fought with myself. Truthfully, this relationship had left me wanting and unfulfilled. But worse yet, for the first time since my childhood someone other than my mother had tapped into my red-hot rage. Glaring, out of control, full-blown nuthouse crazed fury. He masterfully tripped my reptilian brain and I found myself again locked in combat while defending my worth. It left me ashamed of the innate ugliness I hid just beneath my surface.

The waves on Playa Ballena crashed around me in their never-ending ocean symphony, their foaming breakers sparkling white against the backdrop of blue and turquoise water. I watched the tiny sand crabs frantically bolting into their burrows all around my feet. Their intricate sand balls covered Playa Ballena's beach like hundreds of priceless pearls strewn upon the golden sand. The ocean breeze softly stroked my face and I could almost hear Gert whisper his message of love as he patiently walked with me. I imagined his gentle reminder that the oyster creates a stunning gem deep inside its soft tissue from a small grain of irritation.

In the weeks leading up to Costa Rica it was as if the tears I had locked away since I was three arrived overnight. Like monsoon season in the tropics. Sobbing crying. Bawling my eyes out. No makeup left crying. Howling to the moon regardless of its size crying. I could win a crying competition between my divorce and my failed fairytale of love. Huddled on my shower floor frequently, arms tightly wrapped around my knees, I allowed the warm water's cascade to hug my broken heart and muffled my sobs. I sanctioned myself to dwell with my scattered parts and allow it to bleed freely.

I did not start on Day Four. My feet were not able to carry me to the end. I stayed with the group and supported my race friends in their quest to reach the finish line on Day Six. During the celebration dinner on the beach at Drake Bay overlooking the Osa Peninsula, my blood-chilling screams caused much commotion. I flung a blend of flapping wings and countless feet that landed in my lap as far as I could. Much to my chagrin it was only a giant bush cricket (katydid). My Costa Rican friend, Ligia, took my hand and explained the local name was "esperanza," meaning "hope," and it was considered very good luck when one landed in your lap. The jungle had a very eloquent message and a specific messenger to send me home.

The next morning as we sped across Drake Bay by boat back to San Jose, my tears mixed with the wind and ocean spray. Although I left without a medal and a finisher shirt, I brought home something far more rare and extraordinary—the infinite understanding that if I couldn't let go, I would be dragged. I also acknowledged that this relationship unlocked my courage to come face to face with my scissors-fighting younger self.

The Sucking Dating Games

WHEN I TURNED forty-nine years old I reflected on my bleak track record of past love relationships. Tenacity (aka stubbornness) had always served me well. Except when it came to men. *Move on, girlfriend!* wisdom came to me in slow motion. Therefore, once back in Dallas, my jungle clarity faded fast and I went back one more time to him for our last episode of *A Love Dreadfully Doomed*. Yeah, it's rather sad that I liked roller coasters as much as I did. I really needed to get off the ride, hand in my pass, and go home for good. After crashing for the fourth time, I finally did. It was time to try an alternative method in finding my partner and mate.

For most of 2015 and 2016, while willingly trapped at my bar counter writing a memoir, I continued my education about love. About three decades later I still feel like a freshman with a failing grade. I have made some progress and know this is one subject that I will study indefinitely. My breakthrough realizations? Any understanding of this very profound and complex subject would begin with self-love, self-worth, and self-respect. Only when I could accept and love myself first, for exactly who I was, could I find a partnership extraordinaire. Months of self-exploration (and many doses of therapy) later, I realized what no love could ever be: to put the burden on someone else to make me happy, whole, and worthy. Totally genius stuff, don't you agree?

I also felt empowered that I could tell you in fifty-two words or less what I was looking for. By the end of my next book I hope to shrink it to ten words or less. Here goes . . . Instead of a prince and a fairytale to rescue the little abandoned girl from my childhood, I wanted to embrace the authentic woman I had tried to become. I sought a partner, no prince, filled with courage and kindness, to journey forward with me and share the exploration of all that life offers.

How was I to find this creature? Two words. Thirteen letters and one space. Giving up yet? Online dating! I find it somewhat humorous that my Dallas real estate office is in the same building as the headquarters for the online dating service Match.com. I created the screen name Serendipitous, an ode to accidentally being in the right place at the right time. It seemed to be the perfect fit, as I had graduated with honors from the University of Happenstance and Good Luck. When I completed my initial profile with this service and executed my first search, I was treated to a one-of-a-kind response. The pop-up message informed me that after examining approximately 250,000 profiles based on my criteria, no match was found. Wow, talk about ego crushing! Not even one?! As a past computer programmer, I stifled the urge to go upstairs one day while at my office and suggest changes to their search criteria.

Disheartened, I once more turned to nature to guide me in my desire to find a mate. I found my inspiration in a very small set of wings. The hummingbird frequently came to drink nectar from the coral bell-shaped flowers growing on the spikes of my Texas red yucca. Clueless about plants and without a single green finger, I tasked my gardener to install plants that were affordable, hardy, and pretty. In addition to the red yucca, he added Double Knock Out roses to my garden. Their striking cherry red blossoms bring daily doses of happiness and I only regret that I'm not a true gardener to deadhead the flowers faded beyond their prime. I feel guilty and want to apologize to the bushes for my laziness because I sense that I'm missing out on their second bloom.

As I admired the fiery color reflection of my tiny winged friend, I could not help but savor another spectacular example of nature's phenomena. Consider that some hummingbirds weigh less than a US penny but they have the highest metabolism of any animal. I was amazed to think that their oxygen consumption per gram of muscle in flight is almost ten times higher than an elite athlete. I found myself wishing that I could talk to him about hummingbird dating rituals and compare it to our modern order of online dating. Male hummingbirds risk an aerial disaster during a courtship dive, but certainly it must be easier than scanning through hundreds of profiles looking for a human mate.

Let's summarize all the things I hate: being cold, a certain shade of purple, my maiden name, cockroaches, my mother for a while . . . and online dating! It's arguably more painful than the switchbacks on the El Misti volcano and the Himalayan 100-mile race. I'd rather run a desert race barefoot than spend time on a dating site! Although I made strides on my own "worthiness" issues, being rejected and ghosted online makes bleeding race blisters look like the all-you-can-eat buffet on a cruise ship. Not that I will ever be found on a cruise ship. I have seen the Facebook ads and heard the stories from cruise diehards. They are raving fans. In my idea of complete hell, I would be stuck on a seven-day cruise with 3,000 online dating candidates, forced to speed date next to the 24-hour buffet.

You speculate then, why do I bother? Why do I swipe left and right when I despise the concept? Why did I craft a witty profile with twenty-six photos and no selfies? Confession. I want to find him. Blame Disney. Blame the jacaranda legend. Blame all the romantic comedies I watch on the occasion. I am eternally optimistic that my orbit will cross with his. Online, in the grocery aisle, in a hut, a tent, on an airplane, the bush, on a mountain, on a ranch, on a beach, at a race … I'll be ready. Yes, I will!

Recently while in Egypt, I could swear that I'd finally met "the one." When my hands pressed against the glass encasement, I felt as if an electric current had just torched my nerve endings. I did not anticipate falling for a 3,200-year-old Egyptian mummy, but as I stood in front of him in the Egyptian Museum in Cairo, I grasped he was who I was searching for. An ordinary man with extraordinary vision and determination. He bent the will of the world and did not hesitate to create greatness. The force of his presence was not dimmed by the several inches of glass between us or the fact that it was kind of freaky seeing a preserved dead man thousands of years old having this effect on me. His name? Ramses II—the greatest pharaoh and ruler in the history of mankind. I had a full-blown crush on him!

Just months before meeting Ramses II, I was in Hong Kong for a few days. After the Inca shaman's reading of my coca leaves the day before my heart attack in Peru six years earlier, I decided that it was time to obtain a second opinion. I paid a visit to the Wong Tai Sin Temple, dedicated to the Great Immortal Wong, as it was famous for making every request come true. I dutifully bought my Chinese fortune incense sticks, sat at the altar, and made my wish while shaking my bamboo holder as I'd observed others doing. Sadly I didn't realize I was supposed to shake the holder until one stick fell out, which then indicated what wish was granted. Instead I lit and shook all the sticks together! I was confident the Taoists would give me high marks for effort and overlook the rookie mistake. Sigh. As it turns out, I should have explained to Mr. Wong more clearly about the man I aspired to meet. Particularly the part about this great man being *alive* today.

Upon exiting the temple, I invested 300hkd (about $40) to have my palm read by a very old Chinese guy. His price was significantly steeper than the Peruvian currency back in 2009, so my expectations were high. He echoed the Inca man's assurance of a long life and promised much happiness in my future. And . . . drumroll please . . . he promised that I would find the great love of my life! No, he didn't offer a refund voucher in the event that he was wrong! But he seemed very qualified to make such a prediction as he scribbled fancy-looking Chinese characters and referenced a very thick book based on my birth year, day, and hour. I had to lie about my birth hour as I didn't know it. Hopefully it didn't mess up my karma. He folded his scribbles and tucked it into a small red envelope embellished with a wooden Chinese sailing ship and cherry blossoms. I keep it in a drawer in my kitchen to be reminded frequently of the prediction, although I trust that our destiny is largely made up of what we choose to believe.

Finding an ancient Egyptian in modern times is akin to uncovering the Eighth Wonder of the world. But as a steadfast optimist I believe that meeting the man I am destined to spend my life with is imminent. Someone I can love with all my might and call my beloved without any reservation. I want to adore someone not because he is perfect but because he is brave, honest, and willing to be vulnerable. I want to be with someone who would embrace my strength and in return consider me his beloved and cherished. Okay. Okay. I already used up fifty-two words earlier to describe this creature and you are now rolling your eyes. Two more paragraphs and I promise I'll be done. I just want to be as specific as possible, just in case this man happens to stumble across my memoir on Amazon or Audible.

Many years ago I acquired a limited-edition lithograph by Amado M. Pena, the famed Southwestern artist. A man and woman stand within their embrace under falling water. They are draped in a typical Native American blanket and his very large hat allows the water to cascade around them. I can imagine how safe and secure she feels.

I have no doubt that my Creator would never have blessed me with the life I made and not give me a love of such magnitude. I want someone to sit next to me and admire the perfection of hummingbird aerodynamics and be awed by the fact that something so small can migrate from Alaska to Mexico each season. If a person is blind to the beauty within our lives each day, regardless what his profile claims, he won't be my one. And unfortunately, for the present, the online dating criteria do not include a series of queries about hummingbirds, Luxor, or the Valley of the Kings. Yet.

Namaste—The Spirit within Me Sees the Spirit in You

2015 was not my finest year. By midyear my restlessness was ready to burst out of my skin like the Hulk. During the day I sold residential real estate. My nights were punctuated by being my kids' mom, a clandestine wannabe writer, and a budding online dating authority. Single friends sought my advice frequently regarding their dating profiles. Flattered, I briefly considered a side business. Exactly. Agreed. Let's not. But I collected enough material (and still am gathering!) for a follow-up book with the working title, *Looked Good on Paper*.

Stressed on all fronts, my latest DNF from the Costa Rica race (aka quitting) haunted me. It left me once more with a craving to cross a race finish line and be awarded with a medal and T-shirt. I also yearned to explore another untapped region on earth and was burning up with travel fever. My wandering lust made me homesick for all the places I had not been to yet, and my spirit whispered its hunger to be enchanted. As usual, my divine universe delivered! We collided on Wi-Fi during a flight from New York City to Dallas. Southeast Asia in November was "it" and my next race finish line awaited inside a very old wonder: the Angkor Wat temple. The Ancient Khmer Path, 140 miles over six days. In the Cambodian jungle. Nice ring, don't you think?

Bangkok was my first stop—a crazy stew of concrete, gridlock, choking fumes, exceptional humidity, and nonstop noise. Our attraction was instant. While savoring its many wondrous sites I got lost in the sweet seduction of its street food. My last night I sped in a small wooden banana boat down the Chao Phraya river in search of fireflies. In the darkness the large fast-moving barges we shared the narrow waterway with made our boat seem very trivial. My guide spoke only Thai but after several days in the city, my smiles and nods were almost Thai fluent. Forty-five minutes later we turned into a smaller side river and were surrounded by thousands and thousands of fireflies swarming in the mangroves beside the riverbank. Enchanting, their twinkling lights became flickering fairy illuminations reminding me again how nature's formation always surpasses ours. There was no doubt where Christmas tree makers got their inspiration to wrap trees in sparkling lights.

My next stop was Vietnam. After a brief stay in Hanoi I arrived at the bus station in Sa Pa, the mountain region in northern Vietnam near the Chinese border, lugging two large suitcases. What a surprise! I arranged a homestay with a local Red Dao tribal family and was greatly relieved when my host, San May, met me as I got off the bus. She strapped both bags with rubber cords to a small scooter of a friend for transport to her village home in Ta Phin, about eight miles from the town of Sa Pa. We followed my bags on her equally minute scooter. While holding on tightly I admired her competence to maneuver us around cars, trucks, tour buses, eighteen-wheelers, massive potholes, and plenty of livestock along the way. With flashbacks to Indian road mayhem, I closed my eyes often as not to bear witness to our certain death.

We arrived at San May's home just before sunset. It was a very simple wooden structure built per Red Dao tradition and had a mud floor. The wooden slats were loosely nailed together. Without windows, the remaining daylight cast interesting patterns filtered through the openings. The open rafters contained many bags of rice and a few resident pigeons. In one corner, next to a pile of firewood, a simple stone circle in the mud floor designated the cooking area. San May immediately built a fire to prepare our dinner. The kitchen area was in the opposite corner and had a large holding tank with an ongoing trickle of fresh water from the mountain springs. There were two sleep areas, each defined by its own set of wooden slat walls. Although compact without any door, mine had a comfortable sponge mattress and several blankets. The chill already present was a clear reminder that there was no insulation against the cold mountain air. I met the rest of her family, including her ninety-two-year-old grandmother who had come from China as a child! Soon we chatted comfortably while eating our simple but delicious dinner in front of the warming fire.

In addition to being my caretaker, San May was also my trekking guide. In the days following we spent hours exploring and climbing the surrounding mountains. Clouds daily performed their own flirtatious dance of cloaking the valley in wispy white only to retreat, revealing radiant blue skies. Rice terraces marked the mountain face and water buffalo lazily grazed against the steep slopes. Although the dormant rice fields would not be planted until the spring, San May explained that they were kept saturated to be worked easily when planting season arrived. Additionally, the leftover rice plants served as good grazing food for the buffalo. The region had no shortage of water as the streams originated high in the mountains and supplied the villages with plenty of fresh water.

I effortlessly morphed into tribal village life and quickly mastered navigating the steep terrain in the universal rubber slip-on shoes worn by everybody: male, female, young, and old. San May and I became fast friends and I was a fixture among her friends in the village circle of local women embroidering and chatting away. In the evenings I happily squatted next to her on a small wooden stool about six inches from the mud floor while we prepared dinner. I learned several Vietnamese words and phrases as well as the intricate nuances to prepare pho and spring rolls! I had become a member of her family. Despite the Spartan surroundings, the laughter and love around me were as comfy and cozy as a hand-woven blanket.

On my last day they showered me with gifts and presented me with the red headdress the Red Dao women wore. It signified that I was accepted as an honorary member of their tribe. A few hours later San May and I sat next to each other on the steps at the bus station waiting for my three o'clock bus back to Hanoi. No words were necessary and we both avoided looking at the other in a futile effort to dam our tears from spilling. We were an unlikely couple—she was wearing her Red Dao tribal clothes and I was dressed in my Western hiking outfit. The "V" in Vietnam had branded me and left me unwilling to leave my friend and this sanctuary amid the clouds. Three o'clock arrived sooner than either of us wanted. We hugged fiercely. My time in the remote northern mountains of Vietnam was up and blinded by tears, I boarded last.

My final stop before the Ancient Khmer Path race start was in Siem Reap just outside Angkor Wat. Tola, my next homestay host, met me at the Siem Reap airport in Cambodia. With my suitcases we rode in a tuk-tuk to his bamboo hut, my home for the next several days. I was immediately drawn to his gentle voice and the wisdom that I sensed was trapped behind the dark brown pools of his eyes.

I easily blended into another simple village life. We shopped at the local market for fresh produce every morning. His young daughters gleefully showed off their school, the local temple, and the lotus ponds scattered throughout. We ate dinner under the stars while we learned about each other's lives. He sold real estate locally and rehabilitated people who had suffered injuries from landmines still present everywhere. The silent leftovers from a war unimaginable. We philosophized about religion and the evil and goodness in man. But mostly we talked about connection. How its essence was coded in our DNA. No longer just trying to blend in, I fully understood my necessity to intimately relate with those who cross my path. Across countries. Around the world. Rich, poor, frightened, troubled, brave, wise. Together we are imperfect and undeniably human. My chameleon-self had found its home.

Tola shared his own story the next morning over coffee. He was just a young boy when his family was captured by Pol Pot. Slated to be executed, they escaped and fled to the remote village his parents came from. Easily recaptured, his mom and he spent more than a year in prison while witnessing unspeakable horror. To save them, she pretended to be crazy and spoke incoherently. His tears quietly streamed down his cheeks as they lived near the surface and fell without shame. Although his journey was marred by the scars of war, his heart held no anger or hate. He had succeeded in his quest of forgiveness. I told him about my mother. How I didn't strive to forgive. The past was just that—the past. Instead my pursuit was to understand and for it to become a story I could tell without pain. But more importantly, without shame.

A few days later I checked into the race hotel in Phnom Penh. It was Thanksgiving 2015. After breakfast I went to Choeung Ek, the killing fields nearby. A place of such tremendous sadness where evil was tangible. Human courage beside incomprehensible darkness. Religious differences, intolerance for diversity, self-righteous hate, and narrow-mindedness fueled the insanity of peasants. They were the puppets of a madman, Pol Pot. His motto "To Keep You Has No Value, And to Lose You Is No Loss" led to the horrendous deeds of mass genocide.

I was chilled to my being listening to the original screams of the victims mixed with the sirens of the persecutors on the self-guided audio tour. I cried openly next to the Killing Tree where thousands of children lost their lives. I silently sobbed as I stepped around the bone fragments still present and mixed in splinters with the earth. I had traveled from the great temples of Angkor Wat to the massive 203-foot acrylic Buddhist stupa filled with 5,000 human skulls, many cracked and shattered. I bowed my head and offered a wordless prayer to what I held sacred.

I had my Thanksgiving meal across from the Tuol Sleng S-21 Genocide Museum. Unlike the elaborate meal just four years earlier in Prague, it was a simple yet delicious Cambodian dish called Lok Lak, stir-fried marinated beef with a lime, sea salt, and black pepper dipping sauce. Like then I was again by myself far away from home and family. Unlike four years ago, I was not squeezed in a tight ball of anguish. Like then I was crying—but for vastly different reasons.

This time I was mourning the devastating cruelty I had witnessed within the walls of a former high school.

The Ancient Khmer Path endurance start line was now one day away, but its outcome had become irrelevant. My only plan was to walk and run across this land in reverence for a country whose pain and fight for its existence far exceeded my own. I went to these terrible places out of respect for and to understand what my friend Tola overcame. I glimpsed a version of endurance, survival, and courage that filled me with respect. Namaste, dear friend.

Pegasus

ETCHED IN MY MEMORY is the flight of a single flaming arrow to light the cauldron at the 1992 Olympic Games opening ceremonies in Barcelona. Antonio Rebollo, a Paralympic archer from Spain, allowed his arrow, lit by the Olympic torch, to find its perfect arch in the night sky. There was no room for error while millions watched his pullback and release. He had learned two hours before that he was the chosen one from several other archers to participate in the ceremony. I admire his willingness to fail in exchange for inspiring an entire planet to see the perfect union of fire, flight, and light.

I have frequently felt as if the universe decided eons ago to shoot me from its bow on a regular basis. Sometimes for sport, but oftentimes to test my flight and skill. Each occasion taught me better how to stabilize my spin to reach the intended bull's eye. Always choosing my three feathers carefully, I like to pick the peregrine falcon's tail feathers for guidance and control. They have keen vision and when reaching their top diving speeds of 200 miles per hour, they are the fastest-moving creatures on earth. It gives me courage knowing that I have some control whenever I feel the string drawn back just before I'm released to fly. Extreme endurance racing has become my training ground to sharpen my flying abilities.

Why do I hurt myself like this? What part of me enjoys feeling the pain throb through my muscles while my lungs are ripped from my chest? How can I feel pleasure while dressing my blistered, bleeding, and raw feet for another day of running and walking? For five days I had tortured my body to run more than 130 miles through the Cambodian jungle. I had tormented my mind to delve into its reserves not to surrender to the suffocating heat and humidity. To keep moving through the perpetual sandy tracks and over dirt roads. One slow, painful mile at a time. Until the final ten miles on Day Six. The finish line inside the age-old temples at Angkor Wat where I could write "done" next to the 140-mile Ancient Khmer Path.

I traveled far to allow myself the pleasure to soak in my own sweat inside a tent, dressed down to my underwear. For six days my skin was damp as if fighting jungle fever. Each day was blazing hot as hell, stifling and suffocating, torching my lungs with every step. Our route was often lined with village kids handing out small bunches of flowers as the runners passed. They allowed me to drown in the pools of their liquid chocolate-brown eyes. On Day Two I met the person I had come to see. The quitter. The softie. The one I cannot meet in Dallas. She only shows up when the going is a real bitch. On Day Two we negotiated our treaty every mile for every one of the 22.5 miles. She knows my every weakness and almost got me. But my desire to continue was so much greater than her empty promises of relief. Screw her.

It's just pain. A case of mind over matter. Without a shower for days, the grit built under my nails. The forty miles on Day Three were a ruthless exercise in enduring. Fourteen and a half hours later, I had barely the strength to recite my motives for entering the race. Our camp was inside the Beng Mealea temple, built in the twelfth century and site of the *Two Brothers* movie. But I was too exhausted to pay much attention.

Day Four. My silent march to keep moving as the window for quitting had passed. Day Five. Marvelous, astonishing, dazzling Day Five! The running gods strapped little rockets on my feet and I flew across Cambodia. Jet fuel pulsed through my veins and twenty-eight miles later I was amazed! As were the volunteers at the checkpoints.

I washed my feet and arms in a leech-filled pond on Day Two, sat in a river on Day Four, and used wilderness wipes in between. My daily clean were my teeth, underwear, and socks. In camp each night I hardly had enough energy left to pour boiling water over my dinner in a bag. My space collapsed into a very small box of "here and now."

Day Six. The last ten miles to the finish. The day my indomitable wings unfurled and carried me across Angkor Wat. The wings I had to reawaken. The reason I'm willing to endure profound physical and emotional pain. I must see my wingspan and encounter their might when they fly. Their flight comforts me and regrettably, they don't soar when conditions are good.

Soaked in my sweat from all the races over the past five years, my racing bracelets have accompanied me from start to finish. They also witnessed my quitting. One of them is a simple bubblegum pink band stamped with the words "We fight back." Surviving cancer awards you a singular lifetime membership to a club where no application is required. It's a wordless union that bridges stories of fear, uncertainty, courage, faith, and the inevitable question, "How far out?"

During a race it reminds me of the thousands of women who have fought and won their battle. And the many who lost. How I joined their ranks to add "survivor" next to my name. How the potency of pink connected me to strangers with a single hug in the sea of pink at a Komen Race for the Cure. Where the number of fingers we hold up tells how far we came. Pink reminds me to keep hugging each breath ferociously close. Every six months since 2009, I dreaded the drive back to the hospital for yet another "all clear" for six more months. On those days the devil whispered all the terrible "what ifs?" from the safety of my shoulder. Unquestionably the two most useless and wasted words in any language. It has become my mission to rid them from my vocabulary!

I also wear a long, thin strip of leather with the words *Joy, Goodness, Faith, Kindness, Self-Control, Love, Peace, Patience, Gentleness, Forgive* printed repeatedly in gold lettering. It wraps several times around my wrist and has a simple metal clasp. The writing is faded and the leather worn. When I feel it against my skin I'm reminded of Caston. After a hard ride, his sweat-stained bridle rested against his damp skin. Although I held the reins in my hands during those tumultuous days, it was him who gave me comfort. I think of how since then I have learned to fly. I have accepted the disparity that exists between my tender and savage parts. The rewards are large when I can wrap my pain to keep moving forward. Every day.

The Great Deportation Recap

THEY BROUGHT THEIR PLYWOOD, plastic, cardboard boxes, and corrugated metal sheets to assemble their shantytowns. Crudely held together by stones and other loose cinderblocks, their fragmented presence was everywhere, but generally they set up shop on my insides. Most moved in when I was not watching to claim full ownership after years of adverse possession. They found my empty and vacant spaces and I let them take control over my land that used to be wild and untethered.

For years I lived in the shadow of the ugliness that came with the shame of knowing that I was the most unauthentic person I knew. After a while the stench of my own rotting was the menu du jour. The entire house of cards crumbled in 2009 when I was diagnosed with breast cancer and fifty-four days later suffered a heart attack because of a viral infection of my heart. Yeah. Sort of sucked. Still a great T-shirt though.

The universe was kind to tap me on the shoulder twice to get my attention. I do think it overreacted a tad, when one tap would have gotten the job done. The double-hitter was a little extreme. However, I suspect a higher power understood that it had to slap me hard with its best shots. Tasting my own mortality twice during the summer of 2009, like drinking from a rare and priceless vintage, altered everything. How arrogant I had been to take each day for granted. How short-sighted not to gulp every day like a thirsty man finding water after crawling through the desert sand at high noon.

I issued the evictions left and right. The first one was my marriage. We were the most mismatched couple a reality show could dream up. Planets apart? No, try star systems. Great dad and wonderful and kind person—just not matched for this journey. No judgment. Just done.

Next. Stop lying about my childhood. I never was an orphan. Look people in the eye and own the fact that I was abandoned, abused, and neglected. It was not because I had no value or belonged to a group of misfits. She was a bad mother and should never have had children. Certainly not six she could never care for. I booted an entire shanty village by claiming this crap as my own. It was time to build a bonfire and burn the bag.

Father Shed—it was grueling taking it apart. I had dedicated so many resources constructing it in the first place. It had such a far reach in shaping my twisted idea of my identity. Additionally, it also completely distorted my understanding of men to the point I that really thought Disney princes walked among us and that it was my duty to convince them I was worthy of their affection. I'm proud that instead of shelter this shed has become rubble. My mother holds no more authority over me and her letter, like her purple hat, became dust a long time ago. I have no curiosity left about what her truth was regarding my beginning. Instead of dropping the scissors, time gently removed them from my grasp when I wasn't noticing. Whether she lied to me one last time about my father is not important. The love I share with my Makwassie family is not by blood but by a far sturdier tie—our free unqualified choice. Regardless whether Gert was my biological father, he is the only father figure I knew and they are my family. I only wish that my courage to say "I love you" blossomed much earlier.

Mortality Hut—Tough one. I'm not afraid to die. But, to be honest, I'll never be prepared. I cannot tear this one down all the way! But . . . it has become a ten-by-ten pop-up tent for shade against sun and shelter from rain. It fits in my trunk and I'm happy to haul it around and assemble as needed. It's my constant reminder to practice being kind, having compassion, and being mindful. I clearly understand our choice of either living with all our might—or not. Either way, life itself doesn't care which we choose.

I wear my breast cancer badges proudly because they tell my story of persistence. The four-inch-long incision under my arm marks the removal of my first four lymph nodes as part of the sentinel node biopsy. Its line has faded. When I trace its outline across my skin I'm thankful that the small cancer clusters from my first sentinel node were absent in the next three. My ensuing two lumpectomies left behind a dent in my right breast reminiscent of a bite out of an apple. It's now smaller than the left. I find beauty in its imperfection and reconstructing its shape is not necessary.

As I freed up valuable real estate, I allowed joy to take its place. Open, honest, and authentic are the requirements. I refuse to consider any substitutes. Vulnerability and my willingness to accept me as the complete imperfect and worthy creature, are prime. Never again would I cut corners. Love me or leave me. I really don't care. But if you love me, you must love all of me. The good, the bad, the ugly, the quirky, the weird. All of it. Or take a hike. Because no squatting is allowed.

I'm down to my last shack. The oldest one. Circa 1971. My final holdout. "I don't care and it doesn't matter" has shielded my core from hurt since I was a little girl. I have wrapped myself in its loving folds for a very long time. It has been my homey food, like a winter stew, a mellow mutton curry, or my kids' favorite mac & cheese that I make for their birthday parties. Think four cheese sauce, smoked ham, and parmesan bread crumb topping!

But it's time to write this eviction notice. My wildflower meadow cannot flourish if the fright of a winter frost continues to cast its shadow over my heartscape. My beautiful lavender spring will always return. This shed has become obsolete. Let's tear it down. I always cared deeply and it mattered so much to me. Allow me to show you my core. I'm unafraid as I know it's strong enough to withstand the storm.

Amazing grace, how sweet the sound,
That saved a wretch like me.
I once was lost but now I'm found,
Was blind, but now I see.
'twas grace that taught,
my heart to fear.
And grace, my fears relieved.
How precious did that grace appear,
the hour I first believed.

—"AMAZING GRACE," JOHN NEWTON

The Power of Purple

I DRAGGED MY HAND through the water and watched the droplets falling back into the River Nile after it briefly grasped my fingers. The evening breeze gently played with our lateen sails. It allowed our captain to tack against the wind as he guided our felucca across the water. In addition to our sails, the wind teased the folds of my deep purple dress—the exact shade of Mardi Gras and worn by royalty . . . the one I no longer avoid. Like a ripe summer peach, the setting sun against the Cairo skyline invited me to bite into its juicy deliciousness. The last rays reflected off my antique Egyptian silver bracelet that found me in Prague some freezing Thanksgiving night five years before. Sailing on the Nile dressed in purple was my half-century birthday celebration. That morning, in the shadow of the Great Pyramid of Giza, the oldest of the ancient wonders, I felt very young.

Just days earlier, another ageless wonder lay at my feet while tears streamed down my face. My Jordanian guide's request was simple: "Henda, give me your hand, close your eyes, and trust me not to let you fall." I had known Moath for less than two hours, but without hesitation I placed my hand in his and shut my eyes. Although from very different worlds, he and I had already shared our stories while hiking through sandstone mountains. We spoke the same language.

We slowly walked forward together and he instructed me to focus solely on his voice. He painted a vision of being lost in a vast desert—very isolated, thirsty, and afraid. "For days, you have struggled to find your way through sand and over harsh terrain," he softly continued. In his visualization I could see the safety of shelter in a distant cave, but getting there would require me to cross over steep mountain cliffs. "You finally arrive at the entrance only to find it is blocked by a heavy wooden door," he resumed. "You have to push with all your might for it to budge even a little. Inside, a very old man waits. He holds a pure and dazzling white light in his hands." Moath's words mesmerized me. "Now," Moath said as we came to a sudden stop, "as the light gently penetrates your heart, you realize that you have the ability to squeeze every dark spot from your life and let radiance takes its place. Open your eyes, Henda."

I discovered that we stood on the very edge of a high sandstone cliff with Petra's Treasury stretching out far below us. Wondrous, breathtaking, and massive, I was unprepared for the forceful emotion that the sight unleashed. In that moment it was as if I was engulfed by an immense energy older than time itself. My heart disintegrated into a thousand pieces and my soul hovered on the breeze that softly kissed my cheeks. I lingered for a long while at the top of this majestic place resting at my feet while being caressed by the gentle wind and the birdsongs surrounding us. Time was suspended as the greatest sense of peace seeped into my being.

My adventure continued early the next morning to the Wadi Rum desert. Translated as "The Valley of the Moon," its landscape was stolen from a science fiction movie. Across its ocean of fine red sand, hundreds of mountains were created, scattered across like giant floating islands of red, white, pink, and black sandstone and granite rock. No two were alike and many reminded me of giant melting ice cream cones and badly baked cakes whose icing was sliding down their sides. I expected aliens to emerge at any moment and felt as if I had landed on Mars.

I chose a camel as my transport to my overnight Bedouin desert camp. Little did I know that seven hours later my thighs and back would understand firsthand why camels were the ships of the desert. I had frequently suffered unrelenting heat on my races. Child's play! The Wadi midday sun across the shadeless sand roasted me in a hellish hot oven. Hour after hour, at a steady camel pace, I allowed myself to melt into the sun, sand, and the immensity of my surroundings and let my thoughts meander across the expanse. Feeling kinship, I admired the desert animals and plants fighting to thrive and survive in their harsh environment.

I was invited by one of the Bedouin guides to watch the sunset from a nearby area. Known as "The White Desert," it got its name from the stunning formation of large white sandstone mountains nearby. We left our shoes next to the jeep and climbed to the summit in bare feet. The stone allowed me to mold into its crevices for support while its texture gently rubbed my skin like sheets of fine sandpaper. The setting sun invaded my being and washed me in its golden rays. I wished I could always sit on a white sandstone rock and let each day shower me in desert colors. As dusk arrived, Wadi Rum's next act was anxiously waiting to take center stage—the night sky. At first the stars revealed themselves like the shy glance of young lovers. But soon they burst through unrestrained in their shimmer, covering the sky in a sparkling arch from end to end. The Milky Way followed suit by painting its glowing luminous band of more than 400 billion stars overhead.

Sleeping in a tent with the heavenly drama unfolded above? No way! After dinner I dragged my mattress outside. I joined the Bedouin guides to spend the night surrounded by constellations, planets, and shooting stars. I counted at least twenty firing across the sky and each time my demands became simpler. As I drifted off to sleep, filled with intense gratitude, I watched one last flare above my head, completely content to ask for nothing. In the moment I was in full agreement with Neil deGrasse Tyson, my favorite astrophysicist and cosmologist. I knew that the cosmos's atoms were used to create me, its greatness was within me and I was connected to its vastness for eternity. Yes, Ms. Ayn Rand, we are heroic indeed.

Free Dog

I HAD BEEN DEBATING whether to tell you about Free Dog. You may be bored by now hearing another race story. I finally understand the "big one that got away" fishing stories! But I really cannot leave her out of my first book. So you can either read about this amazing creature and the worst PMS story you will ever hear, or you can skip ahead. My advice? For all you dog lovers, keep reading!

As part of my fiftieth birthday celebration, I decided to run a 160-mile race in northern Spain in the Pyrenees over six days called The Way of Legends. Parts of the race were along the historic pilgrimage of Saint James Way to the finish line at the Cathedral of Burgos, a magnificent world heritage site. Many of my race friends from the 2015 Cambodian race in Angkor Wat were present, so it was a small family reunion.

Day One was my usual "show up last" and drown in self-pity at the end because it was a hard day and I was hurting. Day Two rained most of the way and I did surprisingly well considering that I NEVER run when it rains. Still got in last. Day Three dawned bright and breezy and its 29.5 miles were considered one of the easy days as it was mostly flat. Until the PMS beast showed up about halfway between checkpoints at Mile Twelve. Ladies, you know that feeling when you just start sobbing for absolutely no reason? Yup. That was me. I sat on a fallen tree stump next to a dirt trail and cried while praying that the race director would show up in his car so I could quit on the spot.

I dragged my teary ass to the next checkpoint, where I planned to quit. My headspace collapsed completely and I had no courage left to keep moving. Annie, a race friend I had met in the Kalahari race a few years before, was one of the volunteers. Reminder—I quit that race. Annie was also the sweeper for the next checkpoint. Refresher—the sweeper removes the race markers behind the last runner. She wrapped her arm around mine and told me, "Henda, you are not quitting on my watch. I'm walking with you to the next checkpoint six miles away." And she did. I stopped frequently to sob, but we slowly made it to the next checkpoint. She handed me off to Dr. Laura, our medical director and the next sweeper. We covered the next six miles showered in tears, medical advice, and her kindness. She handed me off to Edward, another race buddy from my Kalahari race and the sweeper for the final leg to the finish. Her instructions were simple: "Get her home." And Ed did. It took twelve hours to reach the finish for Stage Three. The villagers and other runners lined the road of the last 100 feet and clapped as I sobbed my way across the finish. It was the single hardest day of any race I had ever done, including the two races I quit.

You can imagine how many people bet on my finishing the long stage of Day Four! Zero—me included. It was the tough mountain stage and we crossed one of the highest peaks in the Pyrenees with an almost 7,000-foot elevation gain. It was about 1:00 P.M. when I left the checkpoint just before the start of the mountain climb. A dog followed me from the checkpoint. As I was unfamiliar with dog breeds, I didn't know that she was an English pointer. I also didn't know how to tell her to turn back to her village we had just left. Half an hour later she was still at my side. I noticed she had a collar and stopped to read her name. It read, "I Am Free Dog."

I was in the middle of Spain, in the mountains, on the Camino de Santiago by myself. And I had a dog next to me with an English name that included "free." Weird. I kept going and she stayed next to me. She never barked. She stopped when I stopped. She ran when I ran. She walked when I walked. She never left my side. When I barfed my lungs out at the summit, she came and rested her head on my lap. She stayed with me for 9.5 hours until we reached the village where the stage finish was. It was on the other side of the mountain and a 45-minute drive by car from her village and our fateful encounter.

Bear in mind, I don't really like dogs. Okay. She was not a dog. The gods sent her to guide me and get me home. I will never forget her. She is the cousin of the whale shark in Belize. Oh, I finished the race, proudly the last runner who didn't withdraw. Thanks to Annie, Dr. Laura, Ed, and Free Dog.

EPILOGUE

My Name Is Grace

SEEN FROM MY REARVIEW, my past is a series of billboards littered across my landscape. Not forgotten, but done. My tomorrows are gift-wrapped to open when I get there. There is no point to getting distracted by their promises too early. Instead my here and now is my present, to relish the sweet joy from my one breath to my next. I have so much, need very little, and want even less.

I saw the sunrise over Mount Everest and Machu Picchu, stood in the rainbow mist of Victoria Falls, and camped at the remote north rim of the Grand Canyon. I witnessed the phenomenon of the Northern Lights' intimate dance with the Arctic. I gazed upon the Taj Mahal, the universal symbol of endless love, and I bared my secrets in the arms of Angkor Wat. Seeking out the wonders of our earth brought me much joy, but it is the small miracles of each day that count the most. I think the universe conspired to gift me Petra, Wadi Rum, and ancient Egypt for my birthday. Seven were just not abundant enough!

My bedside table's crew grew to also include a Nabataean coin from Petra dated more than 2,000 years ago and a solid silver Egyptian ankh, the key of life, with my name spelled in hieroglyphics. At my rate of collection I should consider investing in a larger nightstand soon. All my odds and ends now rest on a small silk-on-silk hand-knotted rug from Saqqara and the shadow of the Step Pyramid of Djoser circa 4,700 years ago. The rug depicts a lotus flower blossoming. My own blooming took the best part of fifty years to sprout from my muck and for my petals to unfold in the sunlight of self-love.

Two weeks before my fiftieth birthday I received the priceless and wondrous reward of a clear MRI, mammogram, and breast exam. It was my seventh year since the summer of 2009 to be cancer free. Afterward I crossed the street to celebrate my promotion to be screened every twelve months instead of every six. You guessed it—my favorite plate of brisket, ribs, coleslaw, and onion rings drizzled with warm barbeque sauce. How much had been altered and how little had changed! Publishing this book is like walking butt-naked through a busy mall at high noon on a Saturday when it is spilling over with people. But like Santiago in Paulo Coelho's *The Alchemist*, once you know you can transform yourself, embarrassment holds no fear or consequence.

I am reminded of life's vitality frequently by the whistled song of my backyard red cardinal. When he flashes his vibrant red plumage on my fence, he reminds me to trust my journey. I want his songful cheer to always accompany me and gently allow all my scars to fade into thin white lines against the backdrop of time. I thank my God for each day, my every blessing, and all the people who make my existence so wondrous. I'm convinced that I shall continue to be shaped into a better version of today. Until I shall find my eternal rest under a Leadwood tree, among the whale sharks in Belize, and along the east shores of White Rock Lake. It's always an excellent place to watch the sunset while sipping fine champagne. My flute is neither full nor empty; instead it's made of exquisite hand-cut crystal. It explodes into a thousand rainbows when the sunrays reflect from its sides. Drinking from such a glass makes it less imperative how much is left.